Sharing *the* Easter Faith *with* Children

CAROLYN C. BROWN

Abingdon Press
Nashville

Library of Congress Cataloging-in-Publication Data

Brown, Carolyn C. (Carolyn Carter), 1947–
  Sharing the Easter faith with children / Carolyn C. Brown.
    p. cm.
  ISBN 0-687-34424-7 (binding: paper : alk. paper)
  1. Easter. 2. Christian education of children. I. Title.
BV55.B76 2005
268′.432—dc22

2005023994

05 06 07 08 09 10 11 12 13 14 —10 9 8 7 6 5 4 3 2 1

MANUFACTURED IN THE UNITED STATES OF AMERICA

Sharing *the* Easter Faith *with* Children

"Carolyn Brown has done it again! As with all of her books, Brown writes clearly and helpfully, with conviction and passion for what and how to share one's faith with children. *Sharing the Easter Faith with Children* is theologically sound, biblically focused, educationally on target, and developmentally appropriate. It should be required reading for every parent, educator, and pastor who wants to communicate and celebrate the Easter faith with children. Brown packs a lot of practical suggestions, insights, and activities into this very readable resource. I am confident children will mature in their understanding and affirmation of the Easter faith when they have been nurtured in families and congregations that take seriously what Brown offers."

Donald Griggs
Teaching Today's Teachers to Teach

Contents

112956

**PART FOUR: LENT–EASTER RESOURCES FOR
CHILDREN AND THEIR ADULTS**

EPILOGUE

Introduction

For Better Or For Worse © 1996 Lynn Johnston Productions. Dist. by Universal Press Syndicate. Reprinted with permission. All rights reserved.

It *is* funny and we are rather impressed by April's attempt to articulate a statement about the meaning of Easter. Behind our laughter, however, is a nervous recognition that we cannot do much better. As one parent put it, "I can manage Christmas. Shepherds, wise men, a baby born in a barn? No problem. But, I do not know what to tell my child about crucifixion and resurrection at Easter. I hardly know what to tell myself about it." The church has not helped this parent too much. All too often congregational plans for Lent focus on adults; services for Holy Week include children only on Palm Sunday and Easter, making no effort to explore with them what happened in between. The assumption is that the children are getting those stories at home and in church school. Unfortunately, parents and even church school teachers, unsure of their message and how to present it effectively to their children, skim over it and even skip it entirely. Since many school systems provide spring breaks around Easter time, it is possible for children to go off to the mountains or beach, munch on chocolate rabbits, and not encounter the biblical Easter story until they are in their teens.

When we do talk to our children about Easter, we face an age gap. For adults Easter means life after death and new life now. Theologians have interpreted the stories with multi-syllabic abstract theological terms. Children, however, are not pint-sized adults. They think and respond to the world in very different ways than adults do. For the youngest and the lucky, death has very little reality. Television cartoon characters who are repeatedly squashed dead only to peel themselves up for further action and fairy tale princesses who are kissed back to life make it hard for children to grasp the finality of death. So Jesus' victory over death is not compelling Good News. Similarly, all of life is new for them. Every day is a journey of discovery. Calls to celebrate new life in Jesus are not particularly interesting. The theological vocabulary of resurrection, salvation, and atonement is too abstract to be meaningfully processed by young brains that have yet to develop the ability for abstract thought.

This does not mean that the Easter message has nothing to offer children. It is as much Good News for them as for adults. But it is Good News for different reasons. It is Good News because God is proven more powerful than any "bad guys" in the universe when Jesus is raised. It is Good News because Jesus is with us always. It is Good News because it shows that God forgives us. At different ages different aspects of this Good News is the Best News for children. Our task is to tell them the stories in ways that are Good News to them where they are and, in the process, lay the foundations for growing understanding and deepening faith.

This book is an attempt to articulate the Easter Good News for children and to suggest ways that congregations can share that message with their children. Part 1 examines the message and the ways children respond to it at different ages. The first chapter is commentary "from a child's point of view" on the Lent–Easter texts from Palm Sunday through Ascension. The second chapter explores children's growing experience of Easter and their understanding of the Easter message from infancy through the elementary years (about age twelve). Part 2 is a series of chapters offering very specific plans for including children in the congregation's Lent–Easter disciplines and celebrations. Part 3 is a collection of session plans to use in exploring the book with groups of parents, teachers, and congregational committees. The final section of the book is an annotated bibliography of Lent–Easter resources for children and the adults who share Lent and Easter with them.

Throughout this book are the invisible fingerprints of the congregations with which I have kept Lent and Easter, with special concern for the children, for the past thirty-five years. Long thoughtful conversations with parents and teachers, wonderful classroom experiences, distressing classroom experiences, worship services planned to include children, and stories shaped and reshaped by many tellings—all became seeds that have grown into this attempt to articulate the Easter faith for children. The staff and parents of First Presbyterian Church, Charlottesville, Virginia, and Trinity Presbyterian Church, Atlanta, Georgia, contributed greatly. Additional fingerprints are those of other educators with whom I have shared ideas in workshops, brainstorming sessions, and desperate phone calls. For all these people and all these experiences I am deeply grateful.

PART ONE

Telling the Easter Story to Children

The Good News for Children: Commentary on the Easter Stories from the Children's Point of View

The stories of Jesus' crucifixion and resurrection are probably the Bible stories we least want to tell children. We prefer to stick with the stories of gentle, kind Jesus who fed the crowds, healed the sick, played with children, and told us to love one another. We want to shield children from the ugly story of how people turned on Jesus and killed him. But no one of any age can get to Easter joy without knowing what happened on Friday. Children who participate in a Palm Sunday processional and return the following Sunday to celebrate Easter joy can only wonder what all the excitement is about.

This chapter is commentary from a child's point of view on the major events from Palm Sunday through Ascension Day. It is an attempt to hear the stories as children hear them, to ask the questions they ask, to identify the meanings they attach to the stories, and to point out truths that are meaningful to adults but beyond the understanding of children. Every child is an individual and will respond to every story in a unique way. Children also grow and mature in their faith on their own individual timetables. Within this variety, however, there are some patterns that help us know what to expect. To give some idea of what to expect during different eras of childhood, I will speak of "young children" to refer to preschool children, "early elementary schoolers" to refer to children in kindergarten through second grade, and "older children" to refer to children in third through fifth grades.

The Palm Sunday Parade

Matthew 21:1-11; Mark 11:1-11; Luke 19:28-40; John 12:12-19

Children read the story of Palm Sunday as welcoming Jesus with a parade. They have experience with celebrity parades (everything from character parades at Disneyland and Christmas parades ending with Santa Claus to parades welcoming home the Super Bowl victors). They march with their scout troops and in bands in hometown parades. Parades are generally fun and exciting. A parade for Jesus looks promising.

The Gospel texts present fairly different accounts of the event. Only Matthew includes children among the participants. Mark and Luke say that only the disciples participated in the parade and that it was fairly low key. In Luke's story there are neither palm branches nor hosannas. John does not mention the search for the donkey. Over the years the church has merged the four stories, overlooked differences, and opted for the triumphal—just as was done with Christmas texts. Most versions of the story for children follow this collective pattern. Indeed, whichever Gospel is read, worshipers of all ages often hear, not that Gospel, but the merged story.

Older children can identify the differences among the Gospel accounts and, in the process, learn to do parallel Gospel study. That is an important exercise, but for a time other than Palm Sunday. On the first day of Holy Week, the focus should be on the big story rather than on learning a Bible study skill.

The Donkey

When reading texts and talking about the animal Jesus rode into Jerusalem that day, follow the lead of modern translations and speak of a donkey rather than an ass (King James Version). Because of current usage of the latter term, children respond with fits of giggles when they hear the word in church. While they are enjoying their knowledge of what the word can mean, they miss the rest of the story.

Children are interested in that donkey. Indeed, many children's versions of Palm Sunday feature the donkey as the narrator telling of his pride and care as he carried King Jesus to Jerusalem. Some children's stories and songs even connect this donkey with the non-scriptural one Mary rode to Bethlehem. Anthropomorphizing the donkey in this way can be a good approach to telling the story to preschool children. First and second graders, however, are trying to differentiate between imaginary characters and historical ones, and so can be confused by a talking donkey in a story the church celebrates as a historical event. Middle elementary children are ready to enlarge their understanding of the day by exploring the significance of a king who rides a donkey.

All four Gospels compare Jesus' arrival on a donkey to the arrival of God's king on a donkey in Zechariah 9:9 (Matthew and John directly; Mark and Luke more subtly). Scholars argue about whether the donkey was a humble beast, the transportation and beast of burden for the poor, or a noble beast used by all people for peaceful purposes. One tradition is that kings rode donkeys in peacetime and horses when at war. In either case, a donkey, unlike a warhorse, is used for peaceful purposes. So, when Jesus rode into Jerusalem on a donkey, he was showing everyone that he came in peace. But, it is also true that in the messianic tradition, of which Zechariah was a part, the messiah was expected to enter Jerusalem riding on a donkey. So Jesus was just as clearly claiming for himself the title of messiah. Claiming to be the messiah was bound to produce conflict rather than peace. Older children tend to be interested in these details about the significance of the donkey.

Hosanna

Hosanna is, for the youngest children, simply a special word to yell to welcome Jesus on Palm Sunday. They join Christians of all ages in their congregation in singing and saying this interesting, happy sounding word to show their love for Jesus. They do not need to know the meaning of the word. Older children, however, are ready to learn its meaning and its Old Testament roots. The phrase comes from Psalm 118:25-26 where the crowds used it to welcome the king to the Temple. It means "Save us now" and recognized the coming king as the only one who could save them from their big problem. It was used to welcome Judas Maccabaeus when he returned victorious from battle to Jerusalem one hundred years before Jesus entered Jerusalem. Unfortunately, the crowd that met Jesus remembered Judas Maccabaeus and thought the Romans were their "big problem." Jesus had other ideas.

What Kind of King?

Discussion of the donkey and "Hosanna!" lead to discussions about the kind of king Jesus was coming to be. The people who welcomed Jesus to Jerusalem compared Jesus to the kings they knew, political kings or the messiah. Children today are most familiar with the kings of fairy tales and ancient history. These kings come on magnificent horses or ride in golden carriages. They do what they want, make all the rules, and are taken care of by everyone else. Their people, on the other hand, bow to the king, obey the king's rules no matter what, and give money to support the king. That is neither bad nor good. It's just the way things are. Jesus comes as a king who rides a borrowed donkey, is kind, forgives when forgiveness is needed, and takes the best care of his people. Rather than fight to claim his rights as king, Jesus is willing to die. Jesus is as different from the kings children know today as he was from the messianic king Jews were expecting!

A royal costume crown and a homemade crown of thorns make good props with which to help children identify the differences in the kind of king who wears each one. Having identified these differences, older children are ready to think about how the disappointment of the crowd when Jesus did not become a warlike king who got rid of the Romans might have led them to call for his crucifixion on Friday. It was the great Palm Sunday Misunderstanding.

Why Did People Want to Kill Jesus?

The first question children ask upon hearing that angry people killed Jesus is "I thought everyone loved Jesus. Why did people want to kill him?" How could the people who welcomed Jesus with a palm parade on Sunday want to kill him on Friday? They need the answer to this question before they can pay much attention to the rest of the Holy Week stories. When one four-year-old asked his assembled class that question, a wise classmate replied, "Because Jesus told them they had to share and they did not want to." He was on the right track.

Jesus made the religious leaders of Jerusalem very angry and uncomfortable. (Note: The most significant thing about these angry leaders is not that they were Jewish, but that they were religious leaders whose authority and vision were being questioned. To avoid suggesting to children that Jews were/are responsible for killing Jesus, use terms like religious leaders or church leaders.) In the Synoptic Gospels (Matthew, Mark, and Luke) the anger of these leaders was roused by things Jesus said and did. John traces their anger to Jesus' claims about who he is. Children understand the very concrete complaints in the Synoptics more quickly than they do the blasphemy charges based on fairly abstract logic in John. So why exactly did the leaders turn on Jesus and which texts help us introduce those reasons to children?

First, **the leaders did not like what Jesus said.** Jesus talked about sharing what you have with others in need. He told people that they were to forgive those who

Why did people want to kill Jesus?	
Jesus Cleanses the Temple	Matthew 21:12-17 Mark 11:15-19 Luke 19:45-48 John 2:13-22
Question About the Greatest Commandment	Matthew 22:34-38 Mark 12:28-34 Luke 10:25-28
Questions About a Wife with Seven Husbands in Resurrection	Matthew 22:23-33 Mark 12:18-27 Luke 20:27-40
Question About Taxes	Matthew 22:15-22 Mark 12:13-17 Luke 20:20-26
Question About Jesus' Authority	Matthew 21:23-27 Mark 11:27-35 Luke 20:1-8
Parable of the Wicked Tenants	Matthew 21:33-45 Mark 12:1-12 Luke 20:9-19
Woes to the Scribes and Pharisees	Matthew 23:1-36 Mark 12:38-40 Luke 20:45-47
Healing on the Sabbath	John 5:1-18 John 9
Anger against Jesus for Blasphemy	John 6:41-66 John 10:31-39
Pharisees' Plot after Jesus Raises Lazarus	John 11:45-53

hurt them. He even insisted that they love instead of hate their enemies. The religious leaders felt this was asking way too much.

Second, **Jesus made friends with the wrong people.** He befriended people no one else would get near. He ate in the home of Zacchaeus, the tax collector, and called Levi, another tax collector, to be one of his twelve disciples. (Tax collectors worked with the occupying Romans and no Jew wanted to have anything to do with them.) He spoke with women, which no man did in public in those days. In this sense, the anger of the leaders was really not all that different from the anger that erupts when a child befriends the class outcast at school.

Third, **Jesus did things that made powerful people angry.** One that children quickly understand was *throwing the money changers out of the Temple.* Most elementary school children are fascinated by this story of "gentle Jesus being destructive at church!" They know they would be in big trouble if they did anything even remotely like what Jesus did.

The entry point to understanding why Jesus was killed is to identify who was angry and why: the Temple leaders and the money changers were angry because Jesus messed up their stuff and told them what they were doing was wrong. Older elementary children are interested in the function of the animal sellers and money changers. They understand Jesus' anger more fully when they know that worshipers could only be sure that the animals they offered for sacrifice would be accepted if they bought them at the Temple and could give offerings only with special coins that could be bought only from the Temple money changers—all for profit. And they share his sense of injustice that the money changers had been allowed to set up shop in the area of the Temple reserved for foreigners to worship. This knowledge helps them understand more fully why Jesus did it. It is important in telling this story to children of any age to include Jesus' punch line: "It is written in the Scriptures that God said, 'My Temple will be called a house of prayer for the people of all nations.' But you have turned it into a hideout for thieves." (Mark 11:17, GNT)

Jesus also angered the religious leaders by breaking their interpretation of religious rules. All four Gospels include accounts of Jesus *healing on the Sabbath.* In John's Gospel, a brief statement about the growing anger against Jesus follows each healing. Younger elementary students, who argue for hours and even come to blows over how the rules of a game were or were not followed, resonate with the religious leaders' anger at one who disregards the rules. It is important to talk through why Jesus healed or did other things that kept the spirit rather than the letter of the Sabbath laws. But at some points of their moral development, children are so focused on the importance of keeping the rules that this conversation will fall on nearly deaf ears. At those times we must simply be content that the children deeply understand what angered the Pharisees and will one day understand how Jesus was interpreting the rules.

Each Gospel also includes texts pointing to reasons Jesus was killed that are harder to explore with children:

The trick questions about *Jesus' authority and which of the seven husbands of one wife will be her husband in the resurrection* make sense to children only as questions that Jesus answered in a way that made the questioners look silly. Children understand that no one wants to look silly in front of a crowd. So, they understand how Jesus' answers would have made his questioners angry. But even children recognize this as petty anger. It may have been the proverbial last straw for Jesus' antagonists, but hardly merited a death sentence. And since the questions about the wife with seven husbands can lead the children of blended families to worry about the fate of their own multipli-married parents in the afterlife, it is best to save these texts for later in life.

Jesus' answer to the question about *the greatest commandment* made the Pharisees angry because it was so good. They asked the question hoping that Jesus would choose one of the many rules and thus upset people who preferred a different rule. But his answer made no one angry. It made everyone think more clearly about the purpose of all the commandments. One popular way to help children understand Jesus' answer is to have them link each of the Ten Commandments to one of Jesus' two great commands. Doing this helps children grasp Jesus' point that the two great commands that all Jews knew were summaries of the ten commands of Moses. Because making this connection does not explain why the Pharisees wanted to kill Jesus, it is best to pursue this study on its own merits rather than to use it as the Gospel writers did to show why people wanted to kill Jesus. It is a good text to share with children early in Lent.

Making sense of *paying taxes to Caesar* requires fairly sophisticated understanding of the interplay of governmental powers and individual responsibilities. Many American children by late elementary school are familiar with the demand for religious freedom. They have learned of it in history classes about the pilgrims' flight from religious persecution in Europe. That provides a base on which to begin exploring the question. But Jesus and his questioners are debating more than religious freedom. So, while the issue can be introduced to children, this is a discussion that will make more sense to them in their adolescent years.

Jesus further offended the religious leaders with the *parable of the wicked tenants* and the *woes to the scribes and Pharisees.* They did not like the parable because they heard Jesus identify them as "wicked tenants" and they certainly did not like the pointed criticisms and name calling in "the woes." While children can understand why the leaders would not like that, they often wonder why Jesus would say things guaranteed to antagonize the leaders. They are constantly warned about the results of saying such things to friends and adults in authority. Exploring Jesus' purpose here requires more sophisticated understanding of the responsibility of religious leaders than children possess. In adolescence they will understand exactly what Jesus was saying, why he was saying it, and how it would have infuriated the leaders.

In summary, Jesus did and said things that angered the religious leaders of his day for some reasons that children can understand. He broke their rules. He "acted out" in the Temple. He associated with unacceptable people. He told the leaders off in public. These are infractions children can understand in the present and which they can grow to understand more fully as they mature.

Counterpoint to All the Angry People: Mary Anoints Jesus

Matthew 26:6-13; Mark 14:3-9; John 12:1-8

In the middle of all the growing anger against Jesus, Matthew, Mark, and John tell the story of a woman who anointed Jesus' feet with costly perfume. Commentators agree that this was simply a beautiful gift of love. The woman (Lazarus and Martha's sister Mary according to Matthew and Mark) gave Jesus the best she had to let him know that he was loved. When she was ridiculed, Jesus defended her and her generous gift. For children this story provides both evidence that a few people (Mary, the women who stayed with Jesus at the foot of the cross, and Joseph who arranged for Jesus' burial) did what they could to take care of Jesus in the middle of the storm and encouragement to follow their example in showing love to those around them.

The Last Supper

The Synoptic Gospels

Matthew 26:17-30; Mark 14:12-26; Luke 22:7-23; John 13–17

The Gospels give us two versions of *the Last Supper*. In the Synoptics the Last Supper is totally focused on the institution of Communion. John gives us a much longer supper with several monologues, but no bread and cup. Children (and most worshipers) focus on the Synoptics' story and are enriched by John's.

For children the whole meal is more "the first Communion" than "the Last Supper." By inviting us to eat bread and drink wine together, Jesus provides us with a way to both remember his life, death, and resurrection and to understand it. Preschoolers begin by simply responding to Jesus' request that we eat bread and drink grape juice to remember him. For them to eat and drink with other Christians is a way to show that we belong to the family of those who love Jesus. Later, when children grasp enough about symbols to understand that a flag stands for a country or a red light means "Stop!" they are ready to hear Jesus identify the bread as his body and the wine as his blood. At that point they begin exploring Jesus' use of bread and wine to interpret his death and resurrection.

As literal thinkers hear the bread and wine identified as the body and blood of Christ for the first time, it is important to reassure them that neither the bread we eat at Communion nor the bread the disciples ate at the Last Supper is actually the body of Christ. It can be helpful to rephrase Jesus, "this bread stands for my body..." or "let this bread remind you of my body...." The same is true for the wine and Christ's blood. There is no magic involved. Eating bread and sharing the cup together are ways to remember and to celebrate what Christ did.

To unpack the meaning of the bread and cup further, children need to begin learning about Passover. First- and second-graders are interested in learning about the holy day Jesus and his disciples were celebrating that last night. They can learn about how Passover was and is celebrated and identify the Exodus story to which it connects. It is important to begin to identify Passover as a holy day Jews and Christians share.

Older children are interested in more and more of the details of the Passover meal. They enjoy sharing in a seder with a Jewish family or being walked through the meal, complete with tastes of the ritual foods, under the leadership of a Jewish adult. With that as background, they are ready to explore the new interpretation Jesus brought to the old feast. Eating matzo bread and drinking wine reminds Jews of the night God passed over all the homes marked with lambs' blood. It was the beginning of their freedom from slavery in Egypt. Eating bread and drinking wine reminds Christians that when Jesus allowed himself to be killed (his body broken, his blood spilled) he ended our slavery to sin.

That Jesus *ended our slavery to sin* is easier to state than to explain to the satisfaction of children. Basically, sin is all that we say and do that comes between God and us. For centuries people had been trying to find ways to get all that sin out of the way so that they could be close to God. They sacrificed valuable crops and animals or gave up pleasures in life to show God how sorry they were about their sins. But none of that ever helped. Jesus came, lived God's love in our presence, allowed our sins to lead to his death, and then forgave us. The crucifixion accounts are filled with stories of Jesus forgiving people around him, even those who were torturing and killing him. Those stories are the illustrations of the broken body and shed blood that make most sense to children.

John's Gospel

John begins his account of the Last Supper, "Now before the festival of the Passover, Jesus knew that his hour had come to depart from this world and go to the Father. Having loved his own who were in the world, he loved them to the end." He then recalls all the ways Jesus spoke of and acted out that love. For John the Last Supper truly is a love feast.

It begins with *Jesus washing the disciples' feet* (John 13:1-20). With only the briefest of reminders about how dirty and smelly feet get and a little information about the first century practice of having a servant wash the feet of guests as they enter a home, children quickly understand what a menial task Jesus had assumed. They can compare it with tasks such as washing dishes, carrying out the garbage, changing a baby's diaper, or cleaning the bathrooms, which no one wants to do today. They can then both enjoy and benefit from rephrasing verses 13-17 replacing references to washing feet with references to today's tasks. "So if I, your Lord and Teacher, have carried out your garbage, you ought to carry out each other's garbage. For I have set you an example...." Children at an early age identify the tasks everyone avoids and consider it proof of their importance to be "above" having to do those tasks. Jesus insists that loving a person means being willing to do whatever needs doing to take care of them.

What Jesus has acted out with a towel he puts into words in verses 34-35, " I give you *a new commandment,* that you love one another. Just as I have loved you, you also should love one another. By this everyone will know that you are my disciples, if you have love for one another." Elementary school children can flesh out this generality by remembering ways Jesus loved people—washing their feet, feeding them with loaves and fish, healing the sick, making friends with lonely people like Zacchaeus, not letting the disciples send the children away, and of course dying on the cross. This can lead to listing ways we can show the same kind of love every day.

Older children are interested in the connection between Jesus' new commandment and the name given the Thursday before Easter, Maundy Thursday. The Latin root of the word *commandment* is "mandate." Thus, the day on which we celebrate the Last Supper is known as Maundy Thursday or you might say Commandment Thursday. It is a day particularly suited to doing things to care for people with needs that are often overlooked.

With John 14:1 Jesus begins a very rich conversation with his disciples. John presents it in lengthy, almost poetic prose that quickly loses most children. But imbedded in it are several ideas that are important to children.

In John 14:1-3 Jesus promises that after death we will be with him and that he is looking forward to that. This is a great comfort to children as well as to adults. We do not know a lot about what happens to us after we die. That is God's secret. But one thing we do know—Jesus promises that we will be with him. Not only that, but Jesus is looking forward to having us with him. We see the beginning of this promise kept when Jesus comes to Mary Magdalene as she is overwhelmed with grief in the garden. Grief is not the last word for her—or for us. When we die, we will be with Jesus, so we are definitely safe.

Jesus continues this theme in John 16 when he says, "I am the vine and you are the branches . . ." How close are we to Jesus? We are as close as a vine and its branches. Not bad.

In John 14:8-11, Jesus and Philip have a conversation about the relationship between God and Jesus that children, who are often confused about this relationship, appreciate. Jesus tells Philip that anyone who has seen him has seen the Father, that everything he says comes from the Father, and that everything that he does is what the Father does. For children "the Father" equals God. It is another way of saying that Jesus is God in human skin. If we, like Philip, want to know what God is like, all we have to do is read about what Jesus was like. Most elementary aged children find this satisfactory despite their literalist questions about who watched over the rest of the world while God was being Jesus. (The answer that God was able to be both present as Jesus in Nazareth and still be on the job as God of the whole world stretches the imagination. But that is appropriate. God is "more" than we can fully understand or describe.)

Following up on his comments about his unity with the Father, Jesus promises the coming of the Holy Spirit who will continue to be God's presence with them. When this is combined with the discussion about Jesus and God, older elementary children find a meaningful collection of ideas about how closely the three persons of the Trinity are bound to each other. It is probably wise to follow the lectionary and save the discussion of this theme until late in the Easter season or on Trinity Sunday. It does little to help children understand Easter.

A single verse that helps children understand the cross is John 15:13, "no one has greater love than this, to lay down one's life for one's friends." One way children begin to understand the crucifixion is that Jesus laid down his life, in order that all people might understand how wide and powerful God's love and forgiveness are.

He let people turn on him, betray him, desert him, torture him, and kill him—and he forgave them and God raised him. It is a very powerful demonstration.

Jesus Is Betrayed and Deserted . . .

Jesus' enemies have been gathering since Palm Sunday. Luke even has Judas consulting with authorities early in the week. But for the most part the betrayals and desertions by Jesus' friends begin to be mentioned during the Last Supper. It is easier for younger children to hear the story of the loving supper and the story of all the desertions separately. Older elementary children can begin to grasp the extra pain for all involved when they realize that some of those betrayals were taking root during the supper. Because they respond so strongly to the desertions by Jesus' friends, these older children also benefit from hearing the abandonment stories told cumulatively.

. . . By Judas

Matthew 26:14-16, 47-50; 27:3-10; Mark 14:10-11, 43-53;
Luke 22:3-6, 47-53; Acts 1:18-19; John 18:1-11

Chief among the betrayers is of course Judas. Children for whom the loyalty of friends is critically important are quite sensitive to how it must have hurt Jesus that it was one of his inner circle of friends who led his enemies to him. Especially the boys need to be reminded that in the Middle East today, as in Jesus' day, men greet each other by kissing each other on both cheeks. Once they know that the kiss was nothing "romantic," children feel the extra sting of Judas' identification code. They, like Christians of all ages, are puzzled about Judas' motives. How could someone who had spent that much time with Jesus have done such a deed? A number of possibilities have been suggested through the years ranging from the possibility that Judas was a greedy thief to the possibility that he was trying to force Jesus to take over political leadership. The fact is that no one knows. All we know is that he did the deed, then was so horrified at what he had done that he hung himself. We help children deal with this and all such overwhelming evil most when we tell them the facts simply and share our amazement at what human beings sometimes do.

. . . By the Disciples

Matthew 26:36-46; Mark 14:32-42; Luke 22:39-46

After supper, Jesus and his disciples went to the garden. Jesus wanted to pray. His prayer shows older elementary children that he was one hundred percent human. Knowing that suffering and death lay ahead, he did what any person would do. He prayed that it not happen, but he also told God that he was ready to do whatever had to be done. Matthew's and Mark's accounts, which leave out Luke's parenthetical details about Jesus sweating "sweat like great drops of blood" and the strengthening angel, keep children focused on the important commitment Jesus kept in the course of that prayer. When exploring that commitment it is easy for adults to slide into moralizing about the importance of obedience, i.e. as Jesus obeyed his father children today should obey theirs. That approach misses the point that is important to children. When Jesus was frightened about doing something very hard, he shared his fears with God, gathered his courage and did what needed to be done. Art that shows Jesus praying hard but in control of himself, and without visiting angels, helps children imagine themselves praying in a tough situation. Jesus in the garden does not abandon his mission.

The disciples do not do so well. When asked to stay awake and pray with Jesus in the garden, they fall asleep once according to Luke, three times according to Matthew and Mark. They mean well, but simply are not able to stay awake with Jesus. Preschool children understand this part of the garden story more than the content of Jesus' prayer. Having tried to stay awake when they are sleepy, all children sympathize with the disciples and are relieved that Jesus is not hard on them. He is just lonely and disappointed. They understand that too.

Once Jesus is arrested, the disciples' desertions move to another level. The sleepy disciples run away. They are afraid the soldiers will arrest them too. Most of them disappear into hiding and will not reappear until Easter Sunday. Peter (according to John) draws his sword to fight. Jesus, with some exasperation, stops him and heals the wounded ear of the high priest's servant. Even Peter, one of his very best friends, does not understand what Jesus has been teaching and showing him for years. Older children can grasp Jesus' disappointment in Peter's violent response to the arrest.

... By Peter

Matthew 26:31-35, 69-75; Mark 14:27-31, 66-72; Luke 22:31-34, 54-62; John 13:36-38; 18:15-18, 25-27

Peter's feistiness gives way to his triple denials later that evening. The story of those denials and Peter's resurrection encounter with Jesus on the beach are, for elementary children, perhaps the most powerful Easter story. They understand Peter's sin and the way it hurt Jesus as he was on the way to his death. Peter, the best friend who had promised to be a friend no matter what the cost, pretends he does not even know Jesus, not once but three times. That is the worst possible way to break a friendship. Most children have some experience with a friend leaving them in the lurch. Many know they have done the same to another friend. The look that passes between Jesus and Peter in Luke's account (22:61) is one they recognize. While they may be able to say self-righteously that they would never turn Jesus in as Judas did, they know all too well about Peter's sin. And most have shed bitter tears over their own experiences in such sinful breaches. Therefore, they value highly the forgiveness Jesus extends to Peter after the resurrection. We will explore that forgiveness more fully in the resurrection commentary.

... By Pilate

Matthew 27:11-26; Mark 15:1-15; Luke 23:1-5, 13-25; John 18:28–19:16

In many ways Pilate was the last of the deserters. Pilate was the Roman governor. He had the power to save Jesus. The Scriptures are clear that he felt Jesus was innocent and wanted to save him. But he was "chicken." He refused to stand up to the crowd and the religious leaders who were intent on killing Jesus. Pilate's sin was that he did not use the power he had to do what he knew was right. The challenge to older elementary children reading Pilate's sad story is to do better with their own power.

... *By God?*

Matthew 27:45-46; Mark 15:33-34; Psalm 22

Finally, Jesus' cry from the cross, "My God, my God, why have you abandoned me," is a cry children understand deeply after hearing of all the desertions. If the physical tortures of crucifixion seem remote to them, the pain of all the desertions is something they understand and with which they empathize. It makes sense to them that these are among Jesus' last words before "It is finished." (Note: Though it is somewhat off the track of the main story, older children appreciate learning that Jesus' cry is the beginning of Psalm 22, which ends with a cry of victory. They learn from Jesus the value of remembering songs or verses that can be a comfort when comfort is really needed.)

The betrayal and desertion stories speak more powerfully to children than do the trials. The trials are complicated affairs in which trumped-up charges are handled in ways that can be understood only with knowledge of first-century justice systems and the ways people can use the rules of any justice system to break those rules. That sophisticated knowledge will come in the adolescent years. It is enough for even older children to know that there were trials, but that they were just shows run by people who had already decided what the verdict would be.

How Did Jesus Die?

Matthew 27:27-56; Mark 15:16-41; Luke 23:26-49; John 19:16-37

Children, even very young ones, can hear and understand the crucifixion story. Preschoolers need to be warned that this is "the saddest story with the happiest ending" or be alerted just before "the scary part" of the longer story about Jesus. Never tell the crucifixion story without concluding with the resurrection. Tell the story simply at first, adding details as children age.

For the youngest, "There were people who did not like Jesus. They were very angry and killed Jesus on a cross. It was a very sad day. Jesus' friends cried and cried. They buried his body in a cave tomb and covered the door with a big rock. When they went back on Sunday morning there was the biggest and best surprise ever. Jesus was alive again!"

Older preschoolers are interested in more details about how he died. Simple, non-gory pictures in storybooks can answer their first questions. Pictures that show Jesus on the cross teach them the basics of crucifixion. The expressions on the faces are important. Sad faces for Jesus and his supporters and angry faces for soldiers and antagonists tell the story to nonreaders. Children often respond to these pictures with deep compassion, wanting to take Jesus off the cross and put his clothes back on him. One four-year-old said that the saddest part of the whole Bible was when Jesus' mommy saw him hanging on the cross.

Older preschoolers are also ready to hear about the loving things Jesus did while dying on the cross. He asked his friend John to take care of his mother. When a thief being crucified with him asked for forgiveness, Jesus granted it. Jesus even asked God to forgive the crowd that arranged his death and was making fun of him while he died. The gentle, kind Jesus of the earlier stories is still himself on the cross when people were being mean to him.

Elementary children get more interested in the details of crucifixion. If they have ever stepped on a nail, they wonder how nails through his hands and feet made Jesus die so quickly. Boys, especially, wonder why Jesus was too weak to carry his cross. They need to hear in a matter of fact way what happened to Jesus.

Roman whips were made of leather strips with jagged pieces of metal tied in the ends. Those pieces would cut into a person leaving deep cuts. Forty lashes with such a whip sometimes killed a person from blood loss. Carrying a heavy, splintery wood cross across your back and shoulder after such a whipping would be almost impossible.

Older children can understand the medical explanation that being suspended with your arms outstretched and the weight of your body hanging on them causes you to slowly suffocate. When the person being crucified tried to push up on his feet in order to breathe better, the nails in the feet caused great pain. It was a horrible death.

Many children neither need nor want this grisly information. Almost none are ready for the long-lasting, brutal reality of the movie *The Passion of the Christ*. But for some children, knowledge of the physical facts about death by crucifixion makes a big difference in their understanding of what Jesus suffered. Upon hearing this information, one ten-year-old boy told his teacher, "Every year at Easter I see this movie at Aunt Ruth's church; it sort of fades out from when Jesus tries to carry the cross. So I figured Jesus was kind of a wimp who couldn't even carry a big piece of wood. But if he took all that whipping and stuff . . . well, he was quite a man, huh?" Knowing the details of crucifixion made a significant difference in his appreciation of everything Jesus did and means.

Older elementary children appreciate the stories in which a few highly unlikely people present at the crucifixion recognized that Jesus was "special." They like that even though Pilate did not have the courage to save Jesus, he did refuse Jesus' enemies' request that he change the "Jesus, King of the Jews" sign posted on the cross. They like that one of the thieves crucified with Jesus defended him from the tongue-lashing he was getting from the other thief—and that Jesus responded to that thief's request for forgiveness. And, they like the story of the centurion (lead soldier) who, having overseen Jesus' brutal execution, concluded that Jesus was indeed the Son of God.

Before leaving the stories of crucifixion, it is necessary to speak of all the theological language the church uses to explain the significance of that event. The Presbyterian Church (U.S.A.) summed it up in the Confession of 1967 (*The Book of Confessions*, par. 9.09) with a statement Christians of many denominations could endorse: "God's reconciling act in Jesus Christ is a mystery which the Scriptures describe in various ways. It is called the sacrifice of a lamb, a shepherd's life given for his sheep, atonement by a priest; again it is the ransom of a slave, payment of debt, vicarious satisfaction of a legal penalty, and victory over the powers of evil. These are expressions of a truth which remains beyond the reach of all theory in the depths of God's love for man."

The fact is that all of these attempts to interpret the crucifixion are more confusing than helpful to children. Because their brains have not yet developed the ability to think in symbols or metaphors, children take the images literally. Because they do not live in a culture in which animals and crops are sacrificed regularly as acts of devotion to gods and governments, sacrificial language is very odd to them. Because they live daily with stories of anthropomorphized animals, killing "the lamb" in order to get forgiveness from God seems terribly unfair to the innocent animal and raises disturbing questions about God. All the sacrifice and redemption of slaves language is intended to emphasize the serious consequences of sin. But for today's children, who may experience forgiveness in their families and are taught to forgive others without "payment," it raises questions about why God must be "paid off" in order to forgive us. Jesus comes off looking OK, but God is again suspect. Therefore, it is best to save this theological language for later. For the childhood years, the stories speak more clearly on their own terms and they lay the foundation for theological reflection in more mature years.

This is especially true when children ask questions that adults answer for themselves with theological symbolism. For example, "Why did God let Jesus get killed?" Conversations based more on the story than theological symbols help children find satisfying-for-now answers. It was people, not God, who wanted to kill Jesus. Just as God does not magically stop people from hurting each other, God did not stop people from killing Jesus. That is just the way God works. Where the conversation goes from here depends on the child. But it generally leads to talk about sin and personal responsibility for what we do. God lets us make choices and does not interfere with the consequences. When we do mean things, people get hurt. God does not stop that. But God does not stop loving us either. Just as Jesus forgave the people who killed him on the cross, God forgives us when we say words and do things that hurt others. That's just the amazing way God's love works.

If one must speak in theological terms to children, probably the most understandable is that of the good shepherd giving his life for his sheep. In this picture Jesus who is "God in human skin" refuses to stop loving people, even when they turn on him and kill him. Jesus, standing for God, is a heroic figure and leads us to conclude, as one pastor tells the children in his church, "God would rather die than stop loving you." This is much more understandable than "Jesus died to save you from your sins."

Jesus Was Buried

Matthew 27:57-61; Mark 15:42-47; Luke 23:50-56; John 19:38-42

To make sense of the details of the Easter story, children need to learn about first-century burial customs in general and how Jesus was buried in particular. For the youngest children, "they wrapped Jesus' body in a sheet, laid it in cave tomb, and rolled a big stone across the door to keep the body safe." The term "cave tomb" connects something they know, a cave, with something they may not know, a tomb. Church school classes that create models of this unusual kind of tomb help children visualize the scene of the Easter story.

The sealing of the tomb and posting soldiers to guard it says to children exactly what Matthew intended when he included it. Jesus was dead, really dead and buried thoroughly. It can be used to point out how completely Jesus' enemies thought they had defeated him. They went home Friday night sure that they were right, Jesus was wrong, and they were rid of him. Celebrating their Friday certainty makes the Easter surprise that much more delightful.

The Easter Stories

The Empty Tomb

Matthew 28:1-10; Mark 16:1-8; Luke 24:1-12; John 20:1-10

The first Easter story to tell young children is the story of the ***empty tomb***. The key message is that God's power beats all the bad powers of the world. On Friday night

Judas, the angry religious leaders, and the Romans thought they had won. Jesus was dead and buried in a sealed cave guarded by soldiers. They had killed him. He would not be saying things and doing things that looked so wrong to them any more. They were right and Jesus was wrong. On Sunday morning at the empty tomb, God proves them wrong. God says, surprise, Jesus is alive. God's power is stronger than any power of any person or group in the world. For preschoolers it is the ultimate "good guys beat the bad guys" story.

The story is very simple and therefore easy to share with young children. On Sunday morning all was quiet with the guards at the sealed tomb. The women came planning to complete Jesus' burial by wrapping good-smelling spices into the sheet around his dead body. That is when the surprises started. The soldiers were gone. The door to the tomb was open. Jesus' body was gone and angels announced that Jesus had risen from the dead.

The key Easter word for preschoolers is "Surprise!" Surprise, Jesus is alive! Surprise, God's love is more powerful than any bad power in the world! For older children, Surprise—God's gentle, self-sacrificing love is stronger than the fighting, killing power of Good Friday.

The key empty tomb verse, beyond the Gospel stories, is Romans 8:38-39, "For I am convinced that neither death, nor life, nor angels, nor rulers, nor things present, nor things to come, nor powers, nor height, nor depth, nor anything else in all creation, will be able to separate us from the love of God in Christ Jesus our Lord." Older children enjoy adding to this list of things that cannot separate us from God's love—nor terrorists, nor bullies, nor family fights, and so on. At the empty tomb, children of all ages celebrate that we are safe within God's unbeatable power. The empty tomb is also a good place for older children to evaluate the different kinds of power used in the Holy Week stories and to ponder those they will use in their lives. Actually for most children, the empty tomb is less about life beyond death and more about God's power.

Most of the Easter symbols, which are often interpreted as symbols of new life, make more sense to children when introduced as surprises. Surprise, inside a brown dead-looking bulb, there is a beautiful flower! Surprise, inside a round hard egg, there is a soft living baby chick! (Or at an Easter egg hunt—surprise—inside an eggshell there is not a yolk, but candy!) Surprise, inside a gray, dead-looking cocoon there is a beautiful butterfly.

According to Mark, the women are so surprised that they tell no one what happened. According to Luke and John, they run to get Peter and John whose responses are also rather confused and muted. Only Matthew tells us that the women left the tomb in fear and great joy to follow Jesus' instructions to tell the disciples to meet Jesus in Galilee. The first response was surprise. The alleluias came later as they began to understand the significance of the surprise.

"How Did It Happen?" and "What Was Jesus Like after Easter?"

Preschoolers will pretty much take the story as presented. Elementary children are curious. They ask "How did it happen?" and "What was Jesus like after he rose from death?" They appreciate the variety of details added by the different Gospel writers. Matthew's story about the guards being posted at the tomb gives the story a sense of reality. They can see how the religious leaders would have demanded that. They also like the fact that seeing the angel of the Lord scared the brave soldiers nearly to death.

(Think of all the other people in the Bible who kept their composure when they met angels.) The power of an earthquake (Matthew 28:2) seems appropriate for the power of the event. They are not surprised that Jesus can appear inside a locked room (John 20:19-20) and disappear at the table in Emmaus (Luke 24:30-31). After all Jesus did some "beyond the usual" things before his death. So one would expect even more once he died and came back to life. They also get the point that, if Jesus could be touched and could eat fish (Luke 24:36-43), he was not a ghost. He was not visiting from the world of the dead. Jesus was as alive as he had ever been, but in a new and different way. Astute older children wonder why Jesus invited the disciples, especially Thomas, to touch him, but instructed Mary not to touch him. There is no satisfying answer to this question. It is just one more question to add to the list of unanswerable questions that are interesting, but not necessarily critical.

The Easter People

Children learn most about the meaning of Easter by exploring the Easter experiences of Mary, Peter, Thomas, and the friends on the road to Emmaus. For each one the empty tomb was not "good news" until they encountered the resurrected Jesus. When they encountered Jesus, they found their world completely transformed in ways that make sense to today's children.

Mary Magdalene

John 20:11-18

Mary Magdalene appears at the tomb on Easter morning in all four Gospels, sometimes with other women, in John's Gospel by herself. Mary is all about loving relationships. Gospel references indicate that she was healed by Jesus ("Mary from whom seven demons had been cast out") and afterwards became a leader among the women who followed and provided for Jesus during his ministry. She had become a very different person as a friend of Jesus. John describes her at the tomb on Sunday morning totally overwhelmed by her grief, grief for Jesus and grief for her own lost life with him. Upon seeing the tomb open, she does not look inside, but assuming Jesus' body has been stolen runs to tell Peter and John. She then returns to the tomb. When she looks inside, she hardly responds to the angels. The resurrection happens for her when Jesus says her name. Jesus is there!

Children come to Easter with widely differing experiences with and comprehension of death. Some have no personal experience with death, not even the death of a pet. For them death is something that happens in stories—and often results in a reversal. The cartoon coyote flattened by a steamroller peels himself off the road. The sleeping princess is kissed back to life by Prince Charming. Video game enemies are killed off without a thought in order to win. Some have experienced the death of a pet and understand more about the finality of death. A few have experienced the death of someone very important in their lives and know firsthand how devastating death can be. This variety of experiences and understanding makes it difficult to speak meaningfully to children about Jesus' victory over death.

Fortunately, Mary Magdalene's story offers a simple concrete illustration that makes sense to all the children and sets the stage for their growing understanding.

While Easter for the groups of women who come to the tomb in other Gospels produces a mixture of fear and joy, John's account of Mary's encounter with Jesus at the Empty tomb produces pure joy. The simplicity of her response makes Mary the woman at the tomb to focus on with young children. Easter happens for Mary when she realizes that death has not ended her relationship with Jesus. She went to the tomb thinking that Jesus was gone. She thought the new life she had known as his friend and follower was over. She felt as if the best part of her had died with him. When Jesus says her name, she learns that though he is not there in the same way he was before (she may not touch him), Jesus is very much alive and close to her. He sees her crying in the garden and calls her by her name. She is not just any woman Jesus met in the garden. She is Mary whom he knows by name. When she and people she loves die, they will still be with Jesus. That is an Easter understanding of death that we can share with children. For children it is not so much a victory over death but what Jesus shows us about death. Just as the risen Jesus still knew Mary and greeted her by name, he knows us by name and will be with us always, even after we die.

One church school curriculum concluded Mary's story this way: "Even though I won't be here on earth, you will know that I am alive because you will see the empty tomb and realize that I have been raised from the dead. And because I live, you will be able to live in a different way than you ever imagined. You will feel like I am part of you just like I am part of God. And I will feel that you are part of me too. The bonds between us will be so strong, you will discover than you can keep my commandments to love and care for each other just as I have loved and cared for each of you." (*The Inviting Word, Younger Elementary Leader's Guide, Year 2,* United Church Press, p. 257.)

Elementary school children are helped to grasp the connection between Mary's Easter experience and all deaths when they hear Mary's story in a cemetery or memorial garden. Church school classes can meet in graveyards or near columbaria on their congregation's property to hear the story. Making rubbings of old tombstone messages about death or memorial garden plaques with messages about death gives the connection between the scripture story and deaths of people today more reality. (Tape tissue paper over the message and rub over it with the side of a colored chalk stick.) Attending Easter sunrise worship services in cemeteries also strengthens the connection and helps children recognize Easter as a real event.

Peter

Peter's Denial: **Matthew 26:31-35, 69-75; Mark 14:27-31, 66-72; Luke 22:31-34, 54-62; John 13:36-38; 18:15-18, 25-27**

Risen Christ Forgives Peter: **John 21:1-19**

The most powerful Easter story for elementary school children is the story of Peter. When they hear it as one story, including both Peter's denials on Thursday and his conversation with the risen Jesus on the beach, children appreciate how huge God's forgiveness is. Peter's sin is the denial of even knowing his best friend. Such a betrayal is the cardinal sin of childhood and one all children understand deeply.

Easter for Peter did not come at the empty tomb on Sunday morning. If anything the empty tomb was bad rather than good news. Peter could only wonder what the Risen Christ would say or do to him after his denials. The usually outspoken Peter is silent during the early encounters with the resurrected Jesus. One can almost imagine the huge knot in his stomach as he slinks to the back of the room each time Jesus appears and his deep embarrassment and fear when Jesus asks him three times whether he loves him. Similarly, one can feel Peter's enormous relief and joy when Jesus welcomes him back as a trusted friend and charges him to take care of others (even though he had not taken care of Jesus). That is Easter joy that makes sense to children. That is forgiveness they value.

Sonja Stewart in *Following Jesus: More about Young Children and Worship* (p. 120) offers the following set of "I wonder" questions to help children grasp what Peter experienced:

...I wonder how Peter feels being with Jesus?
...I wonder how Peter feels when Jesus asks, "Do you love me more than these?"
...I wonder how Peter feels when Jesus said, "Feed my sheep"?
...I wonder how Peter feels following Jesus now?
...I wonder where Jesus is leading him?
...I wonder what kind of "shepherd" Peter will be?

When older children hear this story alongside the stories of Jesus forgiving the thief on the cross and even the crowd that was killing him, the children conclude that if Jesus would forgive all these people, Jesus and God can be counted on to forgive them. This is another case when the stories make more sense and have a greater impact on children than any of the theological explanations of God's forgiving activity on the cross and in the resurrection.

Finally, there is a subtle connection between this story and communion that can enrich the participation of older children in the sacrament. In the ancient Middle East people ate only with their friends. It was a matter of personal safety. Fights could be ended if one party simply invited the other to eat and the invitation was accepted. So, Jesus offered more than breakfast when he invited Peter to share a fish fry on the beach. The conversation that followed confirmed what the meal already offered. Likewise, when we eat and drink at the Lord's Table, we come with Peter to accept forgiveness.

With these stories as background older children are ready to read John's Easter evening story in which Jesus breathes the Holy Spirit on the disciples and gives them the power to forgive also. Just as Jesus forgave, they have the power to forgive those who wrong them. In fact a central mission of the church, according to John, is forgiving people. When this commission is linked with "forgive us our sins as we forgive those who sin against us" in the Lord's Prayer (Ecumenical Version), older children can begin to assume an Easter identity as both the forgiven and the forgivers. That is an important part of the Easter faith.

Doubting(?) Thomas

John 20:24-29

For Mary, Easter happens when Jesus calls her name. For Peter, Easter happens when Jesus forgives him and gives him work to do. For Thomas, Easter happens when his questions are taken seriously by Jesus.

The *doubting Thomas* label misses the truth of the situation. Thomas did not so much doubt that what he had heard was true as he had questions about it. He wanted to see for himself. Elementary school children, especially those who are inquisitive by nature, are relieved to hear Jesus accept his questions. Too often the adults in their lives tire of their questions and urge them simply to accept what is told them. Some adults flat out tell them that to question is to doubt and therefore is "bad." According to this story, Jesus is on the side of the questioners. If Jesus accepted Thomas' questions, they can expect that Jesus, and hence God, will accept theirs. Many who study faith development offer further support for the questioners. They insist that one step on the way to a mature personal faith is analytically questioning what we have been told. Thus Thomas was not running away from belief, but working his way toward belief. When we talk with children about Easter, we do well to listen and encourage rather than to squash their questions.

There is a second, slightly different angle from which children hear Thomas' story. For some reason Thomas was not present when Jesus appeared to the other disciples on Easter evening. Every child who has missed out on something amazing can appreciate Thomas' unhappy refusal to believe them. It was not so much that he did not believe what they said, but that he wanted to see for himself what they had seen. Jesus' response cuts two ways. First, he honors Thomas' wish to see for himself. In effect, he says to Thomas, you wanted to see, so look. I understand. But he continued to point out that others would follow who would believe without actually seeing.

A rotation curriculum from the Presbyterian faith community, Kirk of Kildaire in Cary, North Carolina, suggests that teachers prepare students to hear Thomas' story from either of these angles by setting a large bowl of popcorn in the middle of the room, instructing the children not to touch it, then leaving the room. As soon as the teachers leave, a wildly costumed character enters the room, takes a large helping of popcorn, signals the children to say nothing, then leaves. The teachers then reappear and refuse to believe the children's account of the bizarre visitor until the visitor returns to prove the children correct. Only after the group has talked about what happened does a teacher invite them to hear a similar story that happened to Thomas on the Sunday after Easter.

Jesus Breaks Bread for Two Friends on the Road to Emmaus
Mark 16:12-13; Luke 24:13-35

Throughout his ministry Jesus taught a lot by eating: providing loaves and fishes for a hungry crowd, turning water into wine to keep a wedding party going, eating with Zaccheaus and other outcasts, and of course the Last Supper. Following the resurrection the eating stories continue: eating fish to prove he is not a ghost, providing and sharing in a fish fry on the beach in the process of forgiving Peter, and breaking bread with Cleopas and his friend at the inn in Emmaus.

For children the Emmaus story is less a resurrection story and more a communion story. Preschoolers simply eat Easter bread and recall God's Easter surprise. Elementary school children can see the connection between Jesus' request that they remember him by eating bread together and the disciples' recognition of Jesus when he offered them bread after explaining to them what his death and resurrection meant. At the Last Supper Jesus invented the sacrament. At Emmaus the disciples began living with it and learning from it. On Maundy Thursday children participate in the sacrament remembering all the desertions and Jesus' steadfast forgiveness of the deserters. The Sunday after Easter, children eat bread or participate in the sacrament to remember the Easter surprise.

The oldest children, if they are beginning to learn that communion is a mystery that no one ever understands completely, grasp that participating in communion may lead worshipers to new understandings of God's love. It is a good day for teachers to tell about communion services in which they understood something about God's love in a new way. I often tell children about sharing communion with a local youth group on a mountain in Jamaica. Realizing that these teenagers, who spoke English with a very different accent and lived very different lives from mine, knew the same communion songs I did and felt there was something very special about the sacrament, gave the worldwide family of God a new and deeper reality for me. Other teachers and parents have other stories to tell.

Children of all ages both enjoy and benefit from eating bread together as they read the story. The bread may be a simple loaf broken and distributed among students. Or it may be one of the luscious Easter breads that are an important part of Easter celebrations in Orthodox congregations.

Jesus Sends His Followers Out as Witnesses

Matthew 28:16-20; Mark 16:14-18; Luke 24:36-49; John 20:19-23; Acts 1:6-8

Each of the four Gospels and Acts includes an account of Jesus sending his followers out as witnesses. The accounts vary greatly from John's simple "As the Father sent me, so I send you" (John 20:21) to Matthew's Great Commission to "go into all the world" teaching and baptizing (Matthew 28:19) to Mark's promise of spectacular gifts such as handling poisonous snakes without ill effects (Mark 16:18). John's account in its simplicity is the best choice for young children. Older children, with their growing awareness of the larger world, respond well to Matthew's challenge to tell Jesus' story to the entire world.

The fact that all Gospel writers include this sending forth makes it clear that Christians are not to only hear the story of Jesus. They must share the good news. That makes it important to offer children both the call and child-friendly ways to pass the story on to others. Even preschoolers can make Easter cards that proclaim "Christ is Risen!" to send to friends and relatives. Older children can explore the many ways people can share their faith, from wearing a cross necklace to standing up for Jesus' ways among their friends to raising money for evangelistic efforts. John concludes his Gospel by saying that he has written his Gospel in order that people might believe. That is his way of witnessing. Each hearer is challenged to find his or her own ways of witnessing also.

The Ascension

Mark 16:19-20; Luke 24:50-53; Acts 1:9-11

For children the Ascension provides the answers to the questions, "Where is Jesus now?" and "Why is Jesus not still around if he is still alive?" After forty days, Jesus went to be with God. He promised that he would still be very close. He was not so much going far away as going to another dimension. We would not see him in the way people did before his death or even the way his friends saw him immediately after his resurrection. But he would be close by: "I am with you always, even until the end of the world."

Older children, who are beginning to explore the Trinity, see the Ascension as the point at which Jesus reunites fully with God, the Father. The Holy Spirit then comes as a new way of knowing "God With Us" fifty days later on Pentecost. A systematic theologian may see some problems with this. But for literal thinkers it is a good step along the road to understanding the doctrine of the Trinity.

Summary

Easter is indeed good news for children when it is presented in terms that make sense to them where they are. Easter promises children that God's loving power is greater than any evil power at work in individuals or the universe and invites them to celebrate their safety within that power. Easter promises children that God is with us always—even beyond death. And Easter promises children that God forgives us. One Evangelical Lutheran church school lesson summed it up for eight-to-ten-year olds thusly, "Jesus loves, lives, and forgives."

chapter two

Growing into the Easter Faith: How Children Hear and Claim the Easter Faith from Birth to Age Twelve

Every time we walk through Lent and Easter, we discover fresh meaning—partly as a result of the way the Easter message is presented that year and partly as a result of our particular life situation and changing abilities. This is especially true for children. No parent needs a scientific study to learn that a two-year-old will understand any story differently than will a six-year-old or a twelve-year-old. Still, recent scientific exploration on how children's brains and thought processes develop have clarified those differences and suggest ways we can use our knowledge of them to tell the Passion and Easter stories effectively to children at each age and to include children of various ages in the church's celebrations of those stories. This chapter explores the ways we most effectively share the Easter faith with children from birth to twelve years of age. The chart at the end of the chapter summarizes the content of the chapter and will make more sense after the text is read.

Infants and Toddlers (Birth–18 Months)

Infants and toddlers *learn with their senses*. They see, hear, touch, taste, and smell the world around them and begin organizing what they sense into patterns. We introduce them to Easter by giving them Easter things to see, hear, touch, taste, and smell. We decorate children's spaces at home and nurseries at church. Palm branches and Easter lilies let children see, touch, even smell that something different than usual is happening. Repeatedly playing and singing Easter music, both the music they will hear in the sanctuary and the music they will learn with other young children, begins to build familiarity. Plastic eggshells make great toys for a few weeks and also alert children to something different in their world. Stopping to see church Lenten displays (crosses in the yard, bulletin boards, etc.) introduces even infants to Easter in the same way that viewing a nativity scene introduces them to Christmas. Bringing them to the kitchen at home to smell whatever is cooking for Easter builds a memory bank of interesting, happy smells. Most of all, we introduce the children to Easter with our talk. We talk about the palms and lilies, the music, the eggs, and the pictures. Because the cognitive abilities of children at this age are so limited, it matters less what we say than how we say it. The goal is to communicate joy about Jesus. Key words and phrases to include in conversation are "Jesus," "Jesus is alive!" and "Happy Easter!" The stories come later.

By providing all these Easter things to explore, we are introducing young children to the words, music, and activities that are the language of the celebration of the Easter faith. People who study how young children learn are increasingly aware of how influential the things infants and toddlers hear, see, touch, and smell are to shaping their understanding of the world and their ability to function successfully in it. For example, they begin learning to talk by listening to all the talk around them. Even before they can begin mimicking the sounds they hear, their brains are being patterned by those sounds. So when we surround children with the words, music, symbols, and activities of Easter from their earliest days, we are *patterning them for faith*.

Older Toddlers and Two-Year-Olds (18–36 Months)

The five senses of Easter experiences continue to be important. The infants who played with plastic eggshells now enjoy opening and closing them to reveal things hidden inside. They will make a game of hiding small toys in eggs. If you say "Surprise!" with every opening, you begin teaching them that Easter eggs are surprise eggs. In a year or two, they will connect the surprise eggs with God's surprise at the empty tomb. Decorating classrooms and home with palm branches, Easter lilies, and fresh pictures of Jesus provides opportunities for brief conversations about Jesus. Playing both children's Easter music and sanctuary Easter music continues building familiarity.

The language development that began in infancy moves to a new level of intensity as children begin to use words and even sentences. At this age, children are learning to use words to name things and to tell people what they need and want. Words help them understand and master their world. At Easter they enjoy *learning words and phrases* with which to greet people: "Happy Easter!" "Jesus is alive!" even "Hosanna!" and "Alleluia!" These fun-to-say words focus more on the feelings of the holy season than on the facts of the story and generally elicit a pleased response from people around them.

Toddlers and two-year-olds are ready to *begin hearing some of the Easter stories.* They enjoy the Palm Sunday parade story but do not connect it to the rest of the week. Instead they march around waving palm branches and maybe yelling "Hosanna." The oldest two-year-olds may hear the rest of the story in the simplest of terms: "Jesus was killed on a cross. His friends were so sad. But on Easter God gave them a big surprise. Jesus was alive! They were very, very happy." The feelings shown in the storyteller's voice and face as the story is told communicate more than the words do. Young children follow the emotions rather than the facts of the story. It is important, therefore, to always tell the resurrection whenever telling the crucifixion. The happiness of Easter relieves the sadness of Friday. Actually, most toddlers and two-year-olds do well to understand that people are happy about Jesus. Books featuring simple pictures of Jesus and one or two words on each page offer adults the opportunity to "read" the story, adapting it to each child. The best of these books simply describe Jesus as our very special friend and tell the Passion in only the briefest terms.

During this period children encounter, for the first time, rules and expectations they must meet or face unpleasant consequences. Through very direct experience they learn to come when they are called, to stop what they are doing when they hear "No" or "Stop it," to eat in more and more demanding ways, to use the potty—the list is endless. They learn all this by being rewarded for success and punished for failure. Some of those rewards and punishments are simply praise and correction. Others include little treats and short time-outs or toys briefly denied. In this process, though we do not use the words, we *teach children the pattern of sin and forgiveness* that will be foundational to their understanding of Easter and to their ability to receive God's forgiveness. It is therefore important to model God's forgiveness. There are rules and consequences for breaking them, but forgiveness is possible and throughout the whole sin and forgiveness process, God's love is never in doubt. When we deal with a child who has failed to meet expectations, it is faith-forming to communicate that the action is the problem, not the child. "We don't hit people!" rather than "Bad boy/girl!" It is also important to communicate love once the storm has passed: "I love you, but you cannot hit people." Disciplining a child in this way is as much a discipline for the adults as for the child. It is a discipline that will require both consistent purpose and ever-changing strategies as a child grows up.

Three, Four, and Five-Year-Olds

Three- through five-year-olds (preschoolers) are ready to hear more detailed accounts of the Holy Week events. To the Palm Sunday parade, they can add the stories of the Last Supper, the very basics of Jesus' crucifixion and burial, and the story of Mary at the empty tomb. Feelings continue to be the most important interpreters of the story.

As we tell preschoolers these stories we need to remember that preschoolers are *not as interested in life after death as they are in power.* They want to know who can do what and who is in charge. They are aware of how little power they often have and try to gather more. They want very much to see themselves as powerful people, or at least allied with powerful people. On Easter they celebrate God as the strongest power in the universe and Jesus as the "superest" super hero ever. On Friday it looked as if all the bad guys had won. They killed Jesus and buried his dead body in a tomb that was sealed shut and guarded by soldiers. For two days Jesus' friends hid and cried. Then on Easter Sunday, God raised Jesus and proved once and for all that God's power and Jesus' gentle love are able to defeat any power in the universe. In a world of powers ranging from demanding adults at home to truly threatening child bullies and even terrorists, preschoolers relish finding themselves allied with this powerful God and safely within God's powerful care.

On Palm Sunday, once they have heard the story of the Palm Sunday parade, older preschoolers participate in Palm Sunday parades at church, imagining themselves joining the crowd entering Jerusalem with Jesus. That such a parade was held in his honor makes Jesus seem like an important person to them. So, they happily join the parade to honor Jesus. They enjoy the parades in their classrooms. But when they join older children and adults in a palm-waving processional in the sanctuary, they begin to realize that this is a very important parade indeed.

The Last Supper for preschoolers is all about eating bread and drinking grape juice to remember Jesus. Since most children this age are not yet regulars in the sanctuary, they have limited awareness of communion. There is no need to make that connection yet. For now, prepare them for the experience by telling the story, then sharing a snack of bread and grape juice. As they eat, show kindergarteners familiar pictures of Jesus at his birth, teaching, healing, and so forth, and invite them to tell the story behind each picture. This is a concrete way to remember Jesus. (It also helps children begin to connect the various Jesus stories they have heard to one Jesus.)

The crucifixion is best told to children with increasing detail each year. It begins simply: "People who did not like Jesus killed him on a cross." For some three-year-olds that is enough. With repeated hearings children will want more details. The challenge for adults is choosing the details to add at each age.

Few preschoolers understand the reasons for which people wanted to kill Jesus. All they need to know is that people wanted to kill him. They find this puzzling but accept it as the way things were. The most useful discussions on the topic allow the children to ponder why people would want to kill Jesus. Step in only to correct the blatantly wrong ones.

How did Jesus die on the cross? Books with a non-gory picture of Jesus on the cross satisfy those hearing the story for the first time. Jesus' face and the faces of his friends should be sad. The faces of his enemies should be angry. To the feelings of people at the crucifixion, adults can add, "it hurt a lot" to begin telling that there was pain involved. Two details that add understandable pain for older preschoolers are the crown of thorns and the cruel teasing game the soldiers played with Jesus. Because most children have experience with thorns, they can imagine that having a crown of them pushed down on your head would hurt. Because they play games with blindfolds, they are appropriately offended by the cruelty of blindfolding Jesus then insisting that he guess who had hit him. Don't dwell on these stories; add one at a time simply as detail within the larger story. "The soldiers said, 'If you are God's son, Jesus, you need a crown,' and mushed a crown of thorns on his head. It hurt and made Jesus' head bleed." And "The soldiers blindfolded Jesus then took turns hitting him. 'If you are God's son, tell us who hit you,' they said." Kindergarteners are pleased to hear that while Jesus was on the cross he continued to be the kind Jesus of other stories. He asked John to take care of his mother and forgave the thief beside him. He even forgave the people who were killing him.

Because preschoolers hear every story as a separate story and may not connect them even if they are about people with the same name, *every telling of any of part of the crucifixion story must always be completed with the Easter story.* Without the resurrection, the death of their friend Jesus is an upsetting tragedy. With the Easter ending, it is a wonderful story of God's power in the worst of situations. Older children who are familiar with the whole story can be satisfied with a reminder of what is to come. "(*With a conspiratorial smile*) They thought that was the end of Jesus but we know they were wrong. God had a really big surprise waiting for Sunday morning."

The burial, more than details about the crucifixion, proves to preschoolers that Jesus was dead. The older preschoolers are interested in the story of Jesus' friends wrapping his dead body in a sheet and laying it in a cave tomb. Since few children have much experience with tombs and since Jesus' tomb was different from most current burial places, children need pictures and classroom displays of cave tombs. Burying a doll or puppet in a box cave, then sliding a box "stone" across the opening in the cave, helps these children grasp what happened.

Having heard that Jesus was killed on a cross and buried in a cave tomb, preschoolers are ready to hear about the empty tomb. ***Mary's Easter story*** serves preschoolers on several levels. It is a simple story about one very sad, named follower of Jesus who encountered both the angels at the tomb and the Risen Christ and left very happy. (Do point out that this Mary was not the Mary who was Jesus' mother.) Mary's story includes all the basic details of the empty tomb story and speaks of two things that concern preschoolers most. First, God wins the power contest. Jesus may have been killed on Friday but he rises on Sunday to live forever. To put it bluntly, "Nobody or no thing can kill Jesus or God." God's power and Jesus' power are greater than that of the people who killed Jesus on Friday—and are greater than any other "bad" power ever. That is truth worthy of Easter joy. Secondly, God (with all that power) is with us always. Jesus' presence is the reason for Mary's Easter joy. Even death cannot separate her from Jesus. He is with her wherever she goes and whatever happens. (See chapter 9 for a preschool version of Mary's Easter story.)

At home, *celebrate Holy Week with preschoolers as Jesus Week.* A display of a picture of Jesus, some palm branches, a cross, and a Bible in a prominent location visible to children as well as adults serves as a catalyst for short conversations about Jesus. Also display Easter surprise symbols. Older preschoolers appreciate the surprise that a beautiful lily comes from a brown bulb and that a sweet treat comes in an eggshell (that usually contains a yolk). When we connect those surprises to Mary's surprise when she found the tomb empty and Jesus alive, lilies and eggs become reminders of God's Easter surprise. It is a good week to bring out all the family storybooks about Jesus and add a new one if needed. Reading one story about Jesus each day after a meal or at bedtime helps children focus on Jesus and the coming of Easter. Toward the end of the week, read about the crucifixion and Easter in a single story. It is also a week to try some of the family activities described in the Lenten disciplines chapter (chapter 3).

When children reach this age, we have to make conscious decisions about the place we will give *new clothes and the Easter bunny* in our family celebrations. The adult reason for new clothes on Easter is to celebrate our new life in Christ. This is not a reason preschoolers understand. For them new clothes are simply new clothes. Wearing them takes up the total attention of some children, making it almost impossible for them to pay attention to anything else, and simply aggravates others. There is much to be said for keeping Easter clothing simple and not making a big production of wearing it. (Also remember that Easter classrooms tend to be crowded and the services run longer than usual. Fragile, uncomfortable clothes are likely to be damaged or discarded despite the best efforts of the adults in the room.)

The Easter bunny, Easter baskets, and Easter candy provide another challenge. Though people have tried (in some truly theologically awful ways) to connect the Easter bunny to the biblical Easter story, there simply is no connection. The trick is to keep Jesus rather than the bunny at the center of Easter. Some parents try to banish the bunny, which is increasingly difficult as children hear stories at school and from other children. The more realistic approach is to downplay the bunny and focus on Jesus. Avoid special trips to get photos made with the bunny, bunny decorations around the house, and making a big production of the bunny's visit on Easter morning. Instead provide small baskets with a little candy and hunt Easter eggs, not to see what the bunny left but because hunting eggs is a fun Easter game. Take Easter family pictures on the church grounds to emphasize that Easter is a Jesus Day. See The Church Sponsored Easter Egg Hunt and Easter Sunday chapters (8 and 9) to explore further ways congregations can support parents in keeping Jesus at the center of Easter.

Younger Elementary (Grades 1–2)

As children move toward their sixth or seventh birthday, they enter an era of intense focus on the world beyond themselves. They have gathered enough experience with the realities of the world that they can hear and process a growing amount of factual information. Their brains are developing the ability to categorize and store information and learn skills that focus beyond manipulating items in their immediate world (e.g., adding and reading). In most congregations they are more involved in activities and celebrations beyond their own classrooms. During Lent and Easter, these children are ready to hear more of the biblical stories and to explore their congregation's celebrations of those stories.

Because of their increased experience with the world, first and second graders are ready *to hear with understanding more of the Passion stories.* They celebrate Palm Sunday as old pros and are ready to explore more fully how Jesus came to be killed. They begin gathering a list of people who helped kill Jesus: the religious leaders who did not like what Jesus said and did, Judas who told Jesus' enemies where to find him, and the soldiers who actually carried out the crucifixion. *Crucify* and *crucifixion* are big words for the way Jesus was killed. Because friends are becoming so important, Judas' betrayal and Peter's denial can have big impact, when presented as the stories of friends who let Jesus down. Because children are struggling to understand how rules are made, kept, and broken, and how broken rules bring punishment, forgiveness is an Easter theme that needs to be introduced. It is a good time to tell Peter's story, linking the denials before the crucifixion and Jesus' forgiveness after the resurrection. Because six- and seven-year-olds are more focused on making and keeping rules than on forgiving breaches, they will not appreciate the story as fully now as they will in third or fourth grade. But it is a good story for them to live with and grow into. In later elementary years they will be ready to explore with more understanding what the story says about forgiveness.

Mary's story is still the key resurrection (another big new word!) story. In a world where friends are keenly important, Jesus' calling Mary by name as she wept in the garden is enormously valuable. The first thing the Risen Christ does is assure his sad friend that he is still with her and will be always. The preschooler's Easter joy comes from God's power over those who killed him. First- and second-graders celebrate Easter with Mary, who learned that God and Jesus will be with us always—even beyond death.

Though these children are not yet able to put the Holy Week stories into chronological order, they both enjoy and benefit from exercises that help them *collect the Holy Week stories* they know. One United Methodist curriculum suggests creating a Lenten Tree by decorating a bare branch with stickers that recall Holy Week stories (*Exploring Faith: Middle Elementary,* Spring 2004, Teacher [Nashville: Cokesbury, 2003], 12). On Easter, flowers could be wired onto the branch, thus interpreting the decorations. Resurrection eggs are another way to collect and recall these stories. The commercially available set of such eggs offers a dozen plastic eggs with a Lent or Easter symbol inside each one. Instructions are provided for hunting and then opening the eggs and recalling the stories represented in each one. First and second graders have a hard time recognizing and understandings some of the symbols in these eggs. Parents and teachers can, however, create their own sets of eggs using the stories and symbols with which their children are familiar. A second set of eggs can feature stories beginning with and following the discovery of the empty tomb. It is also a good time to read together Bible story books that include many of the Holy Week stories.

Because children of this age are frequently participating in the congregation's worship for the first time, they have much to *learn about Lent–Easter worship.* They enjoy noting the changing colors and symbols. Point out the purple in the sanctuary, decorate their classroom with purple bulletin boards and streamers, hang a purple banner at home, even wear purple sashes during church school or home devotions—all of these keep the long season alive in the minds of these children. It is also time to begin learning the Lent–Easter hymns of the congregation. With a little preparation and some prompting even non-readers can sing along on at least parts of hymns with repeated phrases or choruses ("All Glory Laud and Honor," "Were You There When They Crucified My Lord?" "Jesus Christ Is Risen Today!").

Because of their story orientation, these children are especially interested in participating in Holy Week worship services that are clearly tied to specific stories. Maundy Thursday worship, during which Communion is celebrated on the very night when Jesus invented it, is quite appealing, especially if it is planned with dramatic readings of the Last Supper story and explanations of communion. When congregations plan for the presence of elementary aged children at this service and clearly invite their families to participate, they provide them a great benefit. (See chapter 6 for suggestions for how to include children in Maundy Thursday worship.) As children grow, they will develop a similar interest in Easter Sunrise services in cemeteries, that put them "on the scene," and even Good Friday services, provided they are not too wordy.

As first and second graders become aware of Lent being kept in the congregation, it is a good time for them to *take on a Lenten discipline with their family.* This can be a challenge for busy families who have done well to celebrate Holy Week for seven days with preschoolers, but it is worth the effort. Choose disciplines with nearly guaranteed success for first attempts. Children who have experience with Advent calendars are prepared to keep a One Great Hour of Sharing calendar or follow a Lenten devotion book. When daily success is harder to imagine, choose one task for the entire season, such as learning the Lord's Prayer as a family. (See chapter 3 for details.)

Older Elementary (Grades 3–5)

Third through fifth graders are able to hear and understand, at least in part, all of the Holy Week stories. Their challenges are to get the stories into chronological order, to explore the significance of the details in the stories, and to clarify their interpretation of the stories. They come to these challenges with brains that are well developed for absorbing and categorizing facts. Their newest ability is the ability to place events in time sequence and in place on maps. We meet them where they are when we help them create Holy Week timelines and maps on which to connect Holy Week events. Since they are doing similar activities at school, doing them at church proves that the Holy Week stories are history rather than "just stories."

Most third through fifth graders face death in much the same way that preschoolers do. Though they have some experience with the death of pets and perhaps older relatives, most older children view death as rather remote. They are curious about death and have absorbed a good bit of the culture's fear of death, but do not hear the Easter message about victory over death as particularly significant good news. Their needs continue to be met by the Easter promise that God is with us—even beyond death.

The Easter message that is wonderful good news for theses children is God's forgiveness. By this time they have enough understanding of and experience with keeping and breaking rules that they recognize their need for forgiveness. *Jesus' forgiveness of Peter's denials* provides them such a familiar scenario that it is the most meaningful Easter story for them. At this age loyal friends are desperately important. Betrayals, desertions, and denials by friends are cardinal sins. Because most older children have searing memories of being both the perpetrator and victim of these sins, they quickly grasp what happened between Peter and Jesus and greatly appreciate Jesus' willingness to not only forgive Peter but to trust him with leadership after his denials. When the story is explored then linked to the other Passion stories of forgiveness, older children understand that the Risen Christ is all about forgiveness. There is no sin, no way they can fail Jesus, so horrible that Jesus will not forgive them and still be their friend. That is good reason for Easter joy. It is also an important truth with which to struggle through the growing freedom to sin that adolescence will bring.

Jesus' insistence that his followers also become forgivers (John 20:21-23) gives these older children a spiritual discipline they have opportunities to practice daily. One way to make forgiveness the focus of Lent is to read this text at the beginning of Lent, connect it to "forgive us our sins as we forgive those who sin against us," and invite children to review each day's sins (both those committed and those suffered) before praying that line of the Lord's Prayer each night at bedtime. Make a clay pretzel to keep near their bed as a good reminder to stick with this discipline. When classes undertake the discipline together, then talk each week about how hard it is to forgive and be forgiven; children are encouraged to acquire this hard-to-cultivate spiritual skill.

The other Easter story third- through fifth-graders particularly appreciate is *the story of Thomas.* They appreciate his intellectual curiosity and his insistence on seeing for himself. His story blesses all their questions—even the unanswerable ones—and promises them that God is not offended by honest questions. It is another story they need to know before entering adolescence, when questioning everything becomes an art form.

Because these children can follow the "big story" as well as all the smaller stories within it, they can begin to *explore themes that weave through the stories.* Probably the easiest is that of Jesus' kingship. They can explore the connections between the kingly parade and welcome on Palm Sunday, the "we have no king but Caesar" on Friday, and the "Jesus, King of the Jews" sign posted on the cross. They can compare the kind of king people wanted and the kind of king Jesus came to be. Young disciples can also explore what it means for them personally to follow a king like Jesus, rather than the usual politically powerful king. Fifth-graders will of course take these conversations to greater depth than third graders can.

Third- through fifth-graders are still *learning their way into the congregation's celebration of Lent and Easter.* The rituals and language are once-a-year events for children, for whom a year is a very long time. Words such as *crucifixion* and *resurrection* need to be practiced and spelled repeatedly. Holy Week, Palm Sunday, Maundy Thursday, Good Friday, and even Easter need to be reintroduced and placed in relation to each other and to the stories every year.

Until this time, children participate in the congregation's worship as a matter of course, learning in the process "how we do things." During the last half of the elementary years children begin participating with a sense of understanding and personal appreciation. With preparation, they receive the ashes on Ash Wednesday and check a mirror later to ascertain that the mark is still there. As they become more self-conscious, they prefer more stylized Palm Sunday processionals carrying their branches just so as they process into the sanctuary with their choir. They imagine themselves at the Last Supper eating bread and sharing the cup with Jesus and his friends. They follow the stories of betrayal and feel the growing darkness that accompanies them in a tenebrae. And, they welcome Easter at sunrise or later in the sanctuary feeling the power of trumpets announcing God's Easter surprise and great forgiveness.

Planning and preparation are the keys to older children's participation in the congregation's Lent–Easter worship. When their choirs sing or some of them read Scripture, or they have been involved in changing the liturgical colors and providing other decorations for the sanctuary, the children are there and engaged. When they have studied and learned, in choir rehearsals and in class, the songs the congregation sings in the sanctuary, they can sing along. At this age the hymns that claim them are storytelling hymns and hymns that speak in concrete terms of the meaning of the season. Repeating a song or piece of a song during worship as a hymn or response helps them claim and be claimed by it.

Just as they participate in Lent–Easter worship with understanding, these children now enjoy *"doing with understanding" Lent–Easter activities* they previously did because it was the Easter thing to do. They have the manual dexterity to draw Christian symbols on eggs and to dye eggs. They enjoy making "empty tomb" cookies to share with younger children and friends and, in the process, recall the surprise theme that was so important in their preschool years. They paint icing crosses on breakfast rolls, knowing the stories from the Middle Ages about hot cross buns. They can even follow the complex directions for folding a palm frond into a cross to display in their room or keep in their Bible during the coming year. All of these hands-on activities are satisfying ways for them to remember the Easter stories and celebrate the Easter good news.

Lent is also a good time for older children to *try their hand at personal disciplines.* Using a book of short, age-appropriate devotions or praying a specific prayer each day are great ways to begin taking responsibility for their own spiritual life. Church school classes can encourage this by choosing a discipline and checking in each Sunday on both the difficulties of keeping to a discipline and the joys it offers. Families can encourage this by choosing a discipline each family member will follow independently and checking in regularly. The goal is that, with six weeks of practice, the new discipline becomes a habit that continues. It is important to discuss this possibility with children at Easter and to be sure they have resources they need to continue keeping the discipline beyond Easter.

For Children of All Ages

As children explore more and more of the biblical stories and begin sharing in their congregation's celebration of Lent and Easter, they are setting the building blocks of their faith in place IF. . . . The big IF is the adults around them. The children are totally dependent on the adults to tell them the stories and welcome them into the congregation's celebrations. Because children ask challenging questions about the story and the celebrations, it is tempting for adults—especially adults who are not clear about their own take on the Easter faith—to skim over both "until the kids are older." This serves neither the children nor the adults. The children are denied an opportunity to begin hearing and claiming the Easter message, and adults (both parents and teachers) miss a chance to stretch their own faith as they share it with their children. The challenge for congregations is, first, to help parents and church school teachers clarify their own Easter faith and, second, to offer practical suggestions about sharing Lent and Easter with the children.

Growing Into Easter

Happy Easter

As children grow into Easter they keep all the meanings and activities they have known at earlier ages and add new ones.

Heart	= the heart of the Easter message for children of each age
Book	= the most significant biblical stories, themes and study activities
Word Bubble	= key Easter words to learn and use
Hand	= meaningful activities for Lent and Easter

18 – 36 MONTHS

Jesus Is Alive!

Palm Sunday

Jesus Is Alive

Happy Easter!

Jesus Is Alive!

PRESCHOOL

God's Easter Surprise

Last Supper

Jesus Killed on Cross

Jesus Buried in Tomb

Mary at the Empty Tomb

YOUNGER ELEMENTARY

God Is With Us Always

Collect Holy Week Stories

Stories from the Cross

Risen Christ Meets Mary

Lent & Holy Week

OLDER ELEMENTARY

God Forgives Us

Peter's Easter Story

Thomas' Easter Story

Timelines and Maps

Follow Themes through Stories

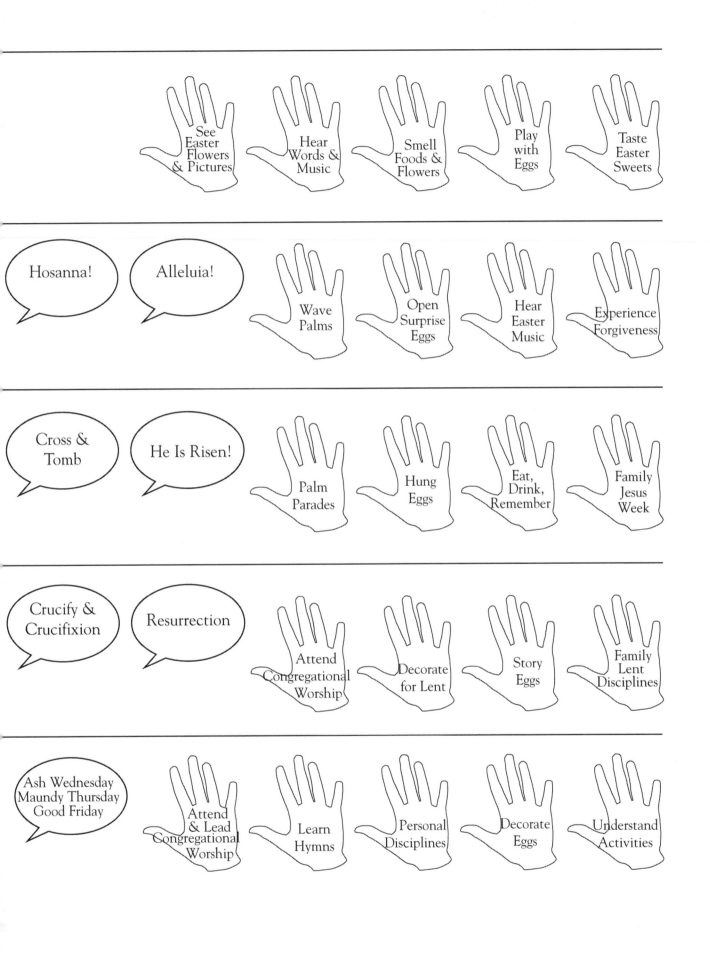

PART TWO

Keeping Lent and Easter with the Congregation and Family

It is important to know what we want to tell our children about Easter as they grow up. It is also important to find ways to celebrate the Easter message, as they understand it, with them over the years. That means families must create and recreate home rituals and disciplines as the children get older. It also means that congregations must plan ways to include children in their celebrations of Lent and Easter. Worship planning teams need to ensure that children are invited to worship around all of the Lent–Easter themes. Mission and education teams need to call children as well as youth and adults to Lenten disciplines. Sometimes this means creating events especially for children and their families. Other times it means planning for their participation and leadership in events for the whole congregation. The following chapters explore ways congregations might rise to the challenges of sharing Lent and Easter effectively with their children.

chapter three

Lenten Disciplines for Children and Their Families

Lent begins on Ash Wednesday and concludes at midnight on Easter morning. It is a time of repentance, that is, of recognizing our sin and making changes to become more what God created us to be. This repentance is undertaken as preparation for Easter. The season lasts for the forty weekdays before Easter. The six Sundays that fall within those forty weekdays are not counted because every Sunday is a little Easter celebrating Jesus' resurrection.

One writer introduces the season of Lent by writing, "Of all the seasons of the Christian's pilgrimage, Lent has probably been most abused. It has in certain times and places become a period of excessive introspection, empty abstinence from tidbits of affluence, and the enjoyment of the gloom of self-denial. Correction of such excesses and distortions does not lie, however, in non-observance of Lent, but rather in the recovery of its rich tradition. The image of forty days as a period of engagement with God, of repentance and prayer is deeply imbedded in Scripture" (*Preaching the New Common Lectionary: Year B—Lent, Holy Week, Easter* by Fred B. Craddock et al. [Nashville: Abingdon Press, 1984], 12). The goal, therefore, in keeping Lent with children is to find ways to "engage them with God" at a new level. It is a time to encourage them to stretch their spiritual wings, to try out new ways of praying, and to serve others in Jesus' name.

One way to do this is to commit ourselves and our children to keeping one or more Lenten disciplines. Lenten disciplines are not the kind of discipline that punishes, but the kind that builds up. They are like practicing a musical instrument or doing exercises that strengthen an athlete's muscles for a sport.

The only Lenten discipline with which many children and adults are familiar is "giving something up for Lent." That "something" is often a favorite food (the "abstinence from tidbits of affluence" quoted above). Originally, fasting was going without food or eating very plain food (no fats, meats, or sweets). The goal was to focus attention on God rather than on making and eating food. The hope was that the fasters would draw closer to God and develop a sense of obedience and humility. As practiced today, fasting often becomes a feat we do to prove ourselves to God and to our friends. It has little to do with engaging ourselves more fully with God. Success tends to breed smugness and failure a sense of worthlessness, especially in children.

It is more in keeping with the spirit of Lent to *give ourselves up to something for Lent.* We can commit ourselves to reading from the Bible each day or to learning the Lord's Prayer or to getting better control of our temper. We can even give up desserts so that we can use that money to feed hungry people. If disciplines that must be practiced daily are daunting, we can commit to several projects to be carried out during Lent, e.g., to gather toys and clothes from our closets and toy shelves for people who need them. The goal is to do something that will remind us of what God values and make us more the people God created us to be.

Older children can undertake a Lenten discipline on their own and, in the process, begin taking responsibility for their own faith. They are more likely to sustain their disciplines if their church school class supports them each week. Most children, however, do better committing to and keeping disciplines with an adult partner. Whole families may undertake a discipline. Or one child and one adult within a larger family may become Lent partners working on a discipline together.

Families that give themselves up to Lenten disciplines help their children grow spiritually and value that growing. Congregations that provide suggestions and resources to parents often make these disciplines possible. Below are a variety of disciplines to which children and their families can commit.

Possible Lenten Disciplines

Prayer

Add a new dimension to your prayer life. Select one simple prayer practice to try for the six weeks of Lent. After six weeks, even with some fits and starts, one often finds that a new practice has become "the way we do things." It is not so important which practice you select as that you select one that looks doable—and give it your best.

If your family does not pray before meals, commit to doing so at one meal a day. Choose the meal that is most likely to be successful for your family. Pray either before or after the meal. The goal is to cultivate a sense of gratitude for the gifts of life, including food and everything else that makes life worth living. Pick one prayer that the family can pray in unison. Or let each person at the table tell one thing they are especially thankful for that day—"Thank you God for Lauren. She is one great friend," or "Thank you God for baseball," even "Thank you God that today is almost over!" Or take turns praying a spontaneous prayer or choosing a prayer from a book. Most bookstores offer one or two children's prayer books. An especially good one for families with younger children is *Thank You for This Food: Action Prayers, Songs, and Blessings for Mealtime* by Debbie Trafton O'Neal. Older children appreciate the section on "For Food" in *365 Children's Prayers: Prayers Old and New for Today and Everyday*, compiled by Carol Watson.

At bedtime, try the traditional prayer practice called *examen.* It is a simple way to think back over the day (to examine it) and talk to God about it. With preschoolers, talk together about the things that were "glad" and "sad" during the day. After the conversation, the adult offers them to God aloud as a prayer with the child folding hands beside the adult. Very quickly children will want to take over, saying what they wish to tell God about the day. Older children will finally want to do it privately.

If children have not yet learned the Lord's Prayer, Lent is a good time to work on it. This can be done in several ways. Pray it together each day. Or go around the family circle with each person saying the next phrase to practice. With older children, focus on one phrase each week. Discuss the meaning of each phrase and use it as a prayer starter for a week, with family members adding related prayers. Turn the whole prayer or each phrase of the prayer into a poster to display prominently as a reminder. Older children could work in the same ways with the Apostles' Creed or any other important statement of faith.

Musical disciples of all ages pray with music. They enjoy selecting a new hymn or song about Jesus to learn. The words can be explored and used in the same ways suggested for the Lord's Prayer. Musicians can sing them and learn to play them on instruments. As a family, select a hymn or song from a hymnal or songbook to learn and sing frequently during Lent. Good discipleship hymns for Lent include "Take My Life" to commit your whole bodies, "Be Thou My Vision," or "Lord I Want to Be a Christian." To sing about Jesus try "Tell Me the Stories of Jesus" with younger elementary musicians. Older children are ready to trace Jesus' whole life by singing "O Sing a Song of Bethlehem," "Go to Dark Gethsemane," or "I Danced in the Morning" and to praise Jesus with the traditional "When Morning Gilds the Skies."

One tasty way to recall your prayer discipline is to banish all snack chips, except pretzels, from the house for Lent. If you look carefully at "classic twisted" pretzels you can see an upper torso with the arms coming together in the center where the hands are folded in prayer. These pretzels were invented in the Middle Ages as a reminder to pray during Lent. Eat them during Lent to remember your specific prayer discipline.

Bible Reading

Become daily Bible readers during Lent. In the Bible, children (and adults) find faith heroes and heroines and directions and inspiration for living. To build familiarity with the Scriptures, commit the family to reading from the Bible each day during Lent. For young children, select a book of Bible stories from which to read each day at bedtime or some other quiet time. If your bedtime ritual already includes reading a storybook, add the Bible story after it to make bedtime "better than ever." Older elementary children are ready to read directly from the Bible. The Contemporary English Version and The Good News Translation are biblical translations created with these children in mind. One simple and satisfying reading plan is to commit to reading one Gospel during Lent. Matthew and Luke are probably the best choices. (Mark is rather short and John is quite abstract.) About half a chapter a day will get the reader through on schedule. Rather than count verses, look at the space a chapter takes on the page and divide it between two of the titled sections. Some chapters are short or tell just one unified story and therefore can be read in one night. A few chapters require three days' reading. An older elementary reader who has successfully completed a Gospel during Lent will be ready after Easter to start on Acts or another Gospel.

Congregations can help families become Bible readers by providing Lenten devotional books designed especially for families with young children. Most of these print an explanatory paragraph for discussion with the text for each day. Creative Communications for the Parish (www.creativecommunications.com or 1-800-325-9414) provides a selection of very inexpensive booklets of such devotions written from a mainline Protestant perspective. More energetic congregations can produce their own reading plans. The preacher may select passages parallel to the sermon texts for the entire congregation to read at home each week. The chosen passages may be listed on a bookmark or in a flyer. (The sample bookmark at the end of this chapter was designed especially for older elementary readers, but with different graphics could serve an entire congregation.)

To get maximum growth for both parents and children, invite parents to work together to create a family Lenten reading plan. One approach is to ask parents to divide the chapters of one Gospel into daily readings. The more challenging, and therefore more interesting, approach is to ask parents to create a list of readings related to one topic, e.g., forgiveness, the two great commandments, or God's presence always. In either case, shortly after Christmas, gather interested parents, perhaps during the church school hour. Explore the selected gospel or theme briefly as adults and parents. Then put the parents to work in teams to (1) divide the chosen Gospel into meaningful sections or (2) using Bible dictionaries, concordances, and word books create a list of Bible readings related to the chosen topic. Once forty-seven texts have been agreed upon, arrange them in an order that makes sense to the group. When the list is complete, print it and distribute it to families to use during Lent. (See the sample "You Are Forgiven So Be A Forgiver" at the end of this chapter.) When this work is done in teams during class time with the promise of no homework, busy parents can be more easily drawn into the project. After Lent, gather the group to share stories about their families' experiences with this discipline. Evaluate the list and identify ways to keep the discipline going.

Mission Skills

Hone mission skills. Jesus' two great commands are to love God and to love people. Prayer and Bible reading help us love God. Trying new ways of loving others is another good way to stretch ourselves spiritually during Lent.

Many denominations sponsor a Lenten offering that supports that denomination's mission work throughout the world. Offering envelopes are provided for adults and coin boxes for children. Some offer a calendar for children to use in gathering their offering. For each day there is a one-sentence description of a way the church uses money to help people and an interesting request to add coins to the box based on a search of your own home. For example, "Refugees often use blankets as tents and to keep warm. Add one cent for every blanket, quilt, and comforter in your house." Responding to these requests builds children's awareness of how much their family has and leads to conversations about the needs of others. Denominational reports show that all these coins add up to significant contributions to the church's work. During busy weeks some families collect their offerings for several days at once. When such calendars are not available from their denominations, congregations can create one of their own.

Projects rather than daily disciplines are good ways for families to grow in their ability to care for others. Select one or more projects for the Lenten season. The list below is only a starter. A local congregation's mission committee could add more related to local missions and even schedule Lenten Loving Projects for Families.

- Share what you have. Fix, clean, and package toys and clothes so they will be nice to get. Add fresh underwear to clothes. Stick new socks in shoes. And pack everything in plastic bags decorated with stickers.
- Go shopping for a hungry family. Most food pantries or banks have a list of what they need to fill an emergency box for a family.
- Invite a lonely person to do something fun with your family.
- Surprise someone with a card or baked treat to let them know their work is appreciated.
- Make and serve a meal for homeless people at a kitchen or shelter. This is not as daunting as it sounds. Most organizations that depend on volunteers for this service provide very simple, clear directions and suggestions. They also have experienced folks on hand to help.
- Give up desserts for a week. Donate all the money you would have spent to the local food bank or pantry.
- Take care of animals. Gather supplies requested by the local animal shelter. Set up bird feeding stations for late winter.
- Become better stewards of God's world by reducing the amount of trash you produce and by recycling. Start a home compost bin for organic waste. Research what can be recycled in your community and start recycling at home.

Keeping the Disciplines

The main thing to remember when undertaking a Lenten discipline is that the times we slip up or fall off the bandwagon are less significant than what we gain by keeping the discipline the best we can. Rather than berating ourselves or our children when we miss a day or let something go, focus on sticking with the discipline today or finding a way to do the missed project tomorrow. The goal is growth not guilt.

It helps to have *a clear beginning point.* Ash Wednesday is the obvious first day for Lenten disciplines. A congregation that does not have Ash Wednesday services that draw families can help those families by making a big deal out of the first Sunday of Lent. Note the changing of the liturgical colors, review congregational plans for keeping the season, commit in prayer to Lenten disciplines, and distribute Lenten calendars, devotional books, etc. Invite all who did not start Lent on Ash Wednesday to enter the season fully on the first Sunday of the season.

It also helps to have *a clear point of completion.* On Easter Sunday morning the focus is, of course, on the resurrection. Find small ways to celebrate how we have grown during Lent. Encourage people of all ages to make Lenten disciplines part of their lives as Easter people.

And it helps to have *reminders to keep us on track as we go through the season.* Families with experience opening the windows of an Advent calendar or lighting an Advent Wreath are prepared to follow similar disciplines during Lent. Lent is almost twice as long as Advent, which makes sticking with it harder. But Lent does not take place during the hyper month of December, which makes keeping it a little easier. To create a tailor-made Lenten calendar do some or all of the following:

- Print the biblical reference for day's reading in each square of a calendar
- Add congregational worship and service events
- Add coin-counting directions to all or a few days
- Select mission project(s) and write it in on the date you plan to do it

- Illustrate the plans with a few drawings, graphics, or stickers
- Post the calendar on the refrigerator door or wherever such important reminders are displayed at home

Families can make their own calendars or congregations can create calendars to distribute to members.

Just as families mark their progress through Advent with an Advent wreath, it is possible to **mark progress through Lent by lighting a candle for each week.** Seven candles (one for each Sunday during Lent and one for Easter) are set in a wooden cross-shaped holder. Families who enjoy live, cut Christmas trees can make the candleholder out of the trunk of their Christmas tree:

- Cut the trunk into two sections, one just less than twice as long as the other.
- Notch the pieces so that they fit together to form a cross that will lie flat on a table.
- Lash, glue, or nail them together.
- Drill seven candleholder holes into the wood, four on the long piece, two on the crosspiece, and one centered on the cross point.

Light the candles each day as you read, pray, or count coins together. Or light the candles once a week on Sundays to mark progress through the season. Because so many families now use artificial Christmas trees, congregations might want to plan to provide the cross candleholders. Perhaps a men's group or youth group would make them.

Another very effective reminder is **a small token to carry** in a purse, pocket, or backpack everyday. Christian bookstores generally carry a variety of small crosses, message coins, and other trinkets that catch our attention every time we see or touch them. Finding one that is perfectly linked to a particular discipline, e.g., plastic praying hands for a prayer discipline, is delightful. But less than obviously connected objects, e.g., a cross for a prayer discipline, will also do the job.

Finally, **a word about keeping Lent with preschoolers.** Six and a half weeks is more time than a preschooler can grasp. It is "forever." For them Holy Week is about as much Lent as they can manage. At home, Holy Week is Jesus Week. A display made up of a picture of Jesus, some palm branches, a cross, and a Bible in a prominent location visible to children as well as adults serves as a catalyst for short conversations about Jesus. Reading storybooks about Jesus alerts children to Jesus and the coming of Easter. Toward the end of the week, read older preschoolers the story about the crucifixion and resurrection in a single story. Try, for this one week, one or more of the disciplines described in this chapter.

You Are Forgiven So Be A Forgiver

Being forgiving is not easy. Forgiving people who hurt us is the hardest work Christians do. Build your forgiveness power this Lent. Read about forgiveness in the Bible. Then practice what you learn about being forgiven and being a forgiver.

ASH WEDNESDAY	Psalm 51:10-11
THURSDAY	Genesis 6:11-22
FRIDAY	Genesis 8:1-22
SATURDAY	Genesis 9:12-17

FIRST WEEK

SUNDAY	Psalm 103:8-12
MONDAY	Luke 15:1-7
TUESDAY	Luke 15:8-10
WEDNESDAY	Luke 15:11-22
THURSDAY	Luke 15:23-32
FRIDAY	Jeremiah 31:33-34
SATURDAY	Psalm 130

SECOND WEEK

SUNDAY	Proverbs 17:9
MONDAY	Genesis 37:1-11
TUESDAY	Genesis 37:12-36
WEDNESDAY	Genesis 41:46-57
THURSDAY	Genesis 45:4-15
FRIDAY	Genesis 50:15-21
SATURDAY	Proverbs 24:29

THIRD WEEK

SUNDAY	Luke 3:2-3
MONDAY	Luke 18:9-14
TUESDAY	1 John 1:8-9
WEDNESDAY	Luke 19:1-10
THURSDAY	Matthew 5:23-24
FRIDAY	Luke 17:3-4
SATURDAY	Psalm 103:2-4

FOURTH WEEK

SUNDAY	Acts 26:9-18
MONDAY	Romans 12:14-18
TUESDAY	Romans 3:23-24
WEDNESDAY	1 Corinthians 13:1-8
THURSDAY	1 Peter 3:9
FRIDAY	Psalm 139:1-6, 23-24
SATURDAY	Psalm 23

FIFTH WEEK

SUNDAY	Matthew 18:21-22
MONDAY	Matthew 5:44-45
TUESDAY	Luke 7:36-50
WEDNESDAY	Matthew 5:38-39
THURSDAY	Mark 2:13-17
FRIDAY	Matthew 6:12
SATURDAY	Matthew 6:14-15

HOLY WEEK

PALM SUNDAY	Mark 11:1-11
MONDAY	Matthew 21:12-17
TUESDAY	Luke 22:31-34, 54-62
WEDNESDAY	John 21:1-19
MAUNDY THURS	Matthew 26:26-29
GOOD FRIDAY	Luke 23:32-34
SATURDAY	Luke 39–43

EASTER SUNDAY   John 20:19-23

chapter four

Ash Wednesday, the Beginning of Lent

For children, Ash Wednesday is first of all the beginning of Lent. It is a way to mark the beginning of Lenten rituals and disciplines. Children appreciate being included in changing paraments and publicly committing themselves to specific Lenten disciplines. Over time they come to understand the significance of the ashes. They, however, have difficulty grasping the language about sin and death that is used in the liturgies of most books of common worship, and only grow to comprehend the Ash Wednesday acknowledgement of the pervasiveness of sin when they are much older. Therefore, the challenge to including children in Ash Wednesday worship is to both meet them where they are and expose them to what they can only begin to understand.

The starting point is highlighting the beginning of Lent. Children like recognizing the things that make Lent different and enjoy participating in making those changes. Changing the paraments to purple and hanging Lenten banners can be pointed out during, or actually done, during Ash Wednesday worship; or children can help make the changes before the worship service.

Some congregations ban the use of the word "alleluia" in worship during Lent. One way to mark this practice is to "bury the alleluia." The word alleluia is printed on a small poster and beautifully decorated. During worship, the poster is ceremoniously put in a box or hidden somewhere in the sanctuary. It is then brought out with fanfare on Easter morning.

The lectionary texts for Ash Wednesday focus on sin, repentance, and forgiveness in rather abstract theological terms. The biblical stories about Noah's forty days on the ark, forty years of Exodus in the wilderness, and Jesus' forty days in the desert speak more helpfully to children focused on the beginning of Lent. On the first of the forty days of Lent, we are invited to participate in the biblical seasons of forty. In Noah's time God was cleaning out all the sin that mucked up the world. We are invited to clean the sin out of our lives. As they traveled through the wilderness for forty years, the Hebrew ex-slaves learned to live as God's free people. We are invited to live more like God's people today. As he fasted in the desert, Jesus clarified his mission and dismissed the temptations. We are invited to understand more fully our own missions and what it means to be Jesus' disciples.

For most children sin is the bad things we do and sinners are the people who do bad things. Because adults tell them forcefully and frequently that they are able to choose not to do sinful acts and that they need not be sinners, the Ash Wednesday focus on the pervasiveness of sin does not make much sense to them. Because adults encourage them to be responsible for themselves and not follow others, their complicity in social and institutional sin is a hard sell. Participating in Ash Wednesday worship and observing adults confess their sinfulness can, however, over the years, stretch a child's understanding. At first it is simply amazing for them to see adults whom they respect and know to be respected in their community wearing ashes on their foreheads. They often begin to understand the ashes by focusing on their cross shape. Wearing the ashes is a way of saying "I am a Christian. I belong to Jesus who died on a cross and rose again." They join their parents, teachers, and community leaders wearing the ashes to say, "See, I am one of them too, I am just like...." Over the years they have to cope with the fact that the mark of the cross is drawn not with a golden marker, but with ashes. To be a Christian is to admit to sin. Telling older elementary children that the ashes are made by burning palms from last Palm Sunday, even making those ashes in the children's presence, helps them begin to understand the breadth of sin in all our lives.

Ash Wednesday is an appropriate day to explore the meaning of repentance with children. On Ash Wednesday we confess our sins. We also commit ourselves to doing what we can to change our ways. Lent becomes spring training for repenters.

Communion on Ash Wednesday is food for the season. Especially as we recognize our sinfulness and commit to a season of repentance, we eat bread and share the cup to remind ourselves that God loves us always, no matter how sinful we may be or how we fall short of keeping our Lenten disciplines. The bread and wine of communion are the training table of Lent.

Ash Wednesday Worship Plan

It is often easier for families with school-age children to participate in weekday evening worship when a meal is included. Ash Wednesday worship lends itself to two kinds of meals. One is a simple Lenten soup and salad meal with peanut butter and jelly sandwich makings for children who need that. If possible set up long tables in the shape of a cross with loaves of bread, a communion chalice and open Bible placed at the intersection. Leave an empty chair at the head of the cross for Jesus. If more seating is needed, place long tables in parallel rows at the foot of the cross tables or in a border around the cross tables.

The other meal is a pancake supper to celebrate Shrove Tuesday followed by an Ash Wednesday service. Pull out all the stops with bacon, rich pancakes, butter, syrup, fruit toppings, even whipped cream. Serve orange juice, milk, and good coffee. Set tables with Mardi Gras colors (purple, green, and gold) in the tablecloths, napkins, and streamers down the middle of the tables. At the conclusion of the meal, explain briefly the reason for eating pancakes just before Lent and the changes that come with Lent. Involve everyone in cleaning up the tables, returning all extra food to the kitchen, rolling up the trash and Mardi Gras decorations in the disposable tablecloths to put in handy trash and storage bins. If worship is to take place around the tables, give each table a white paper or plastic cloth to spread over their empty table. Bring to each table any Lenten symbols that serve as a centerpiece for the worship service, e.g., loaf of bread and chalice, a cross. If worship is to take place in the sanctuary, leave the dining hall in a processional. If your congregation has hand-bells, ask ringers to toll them along the way to the sanctuary. School-age children, especially older ones, enjoy this two-part experience. Preschoolers, however, have difficulty making the required change of mood from Mardi Gras to Ash Wednesday and therefore are best served with loving childcare for even a brief Ash Wednesday worship service when it follows a festive pancake supper.

Outlines for two Ash Wednesday services follow. The first is a more traditional service that probably takes place in the sanctuary and includes the imposition of ashes and possibly Holy Communion. The second may take place in either the sanctuary or around tables in the fellowship hall and is briefer and more focused on the beginning of Lent than on confession of sin.

Traditional Ash Wednesday Service with Imposition of Ashes

A good case could be made for declaring Peter the patron saint of Ash Wednesday. Accounts of his life are filled with courageous leadership and embarrassing sinful failings. No matter what happened, Peter faced up to what he had done and repented when he needed to. The heart of this service is retelling some of Peter's stories so that worshipers might identify with both his sin and his repentance.

The resources below are the raw materials from which both fairly formal and rather informal orders of worship can be constructed. The service begins with a call to worship and confession. Before the assurance of pardon is stated, the preacher leads the congregation in exploring Peter's experiences with sin and repentance. Ashes are imposed as admission that, like Peter, we are all sinners and need to repent. Only then is the assurance of pardon pronounced. With that pronouncement the focus shifts to the beginning of Lenten repentance. The paraments are changed in the sanctuary. Possible Lenten disciplines are suggested and materials to support them are provided. The offering becomes an offering of commitments to Lenten disciplines. Communion may then be celebrated as the food for repentance. The closing hymn is one of commitment.

Call to Worship

Soloist sings first verse of "Let All Mortal Flesh Keep Silence"

Call to Confession

(Leader) As we gather for worship on this Ash Wednesday, if we say we have no sin, we deceive ourselves, and the truth is not in us. But if we confess our sins, God who is faithful and just will forgive us our sins and cleanse us from all unrighteousness. In humility and faith let us confess our sin to God.

Prayer of Confession (All in Unison)

Merciful God, we confess that we have sinned against you
   in thought, word, and deed,
   by what we have done,
   and by what we have left undone.
We have not loved you with our whole heart and mind and strength.
   We have not loved our neighbors as ourselves.

In your mercy forgive what we have been,
    help us amend what we are,
    and direct what we shall be,
    so that we may delight in your will
    and walk in your ways,
    to the glory of your holy name.

Hymn   "Open My Eyes That I May See"

Scriptures and Meditation on Peter's Sin and Repentance

The preacher may offer a traditional sermon based on one or two of the stories about Peter. Or, in order to present more of the stories about Peter, a reader might read each story with the preacher speaking after each story to offer reflections on that story and build on the theme of Peter's sin and repentance. The texts below have been pared for brevity and the focus of children. Worship planners should select three or four of them at most.

- Luke 5:4-11 (Peter is called by Jesus and says that he is a sinner)
- Matthew 14:22-32 (Peter steps out of the boat and sinks)
- Matthew 18:21-22 (Peter asks, "How many times shall I forgive?" and is surprised by Jesus' answer)
- Mark 8:27-33 (Peter understands Jesus is the Christ, but not Jesus' words "I will suffer")
- Mark 14:27-31 and John 21:3-8a, 12-13, 14-19 (Peter denies Jesus and is forgiven)
- Matthew 16:18-19 (Jesus calls Peter [and all like him] the "rock" upon which the church is built)

Imposition of Ashes

Assurance of Pardon

(Leader) Hear the good news! Who is in a position to condemn? Only Christ, and Christ died for us, Christ rose for us, Christ reigns in power for us, Christ prays for us.

Anyone who is in Christ is a new creation. The old life has gone; a new life has begun. Know that you are forgiven and be at peace. Amen.

A Call to Repentance (Changing the Paraments)

Change the paraments, even large dossal cloths and banners. This may done in a very structured way with one team removing the green paraments and a second team processing in with and installing purple paraments. (Teams should include worshipers of all ages, maybe families.) Ladders can be used as needed. Music may be played as worshipers watch the action. Or the process may be more informal with a speaker explaining the meaning of the items being removed and added.

Offering of Lenten Disciplines

Direct worshipers to devotional materials, calendars of Lenten activities, offering envelopes, coin boxes, etc. Conclude with prayers committing to the work of repenting in our private lives and in the larger world.

Celebration of Holy Communion

If communion is celebrated during this service, celebrate it as the food of God's grace for the work of repentance.

Hymn "Take My Life and Let It Be Consecrated"

Charge and Benediction

A Family Ash Wednesday Worship: Getting Ready to Bear Crosses

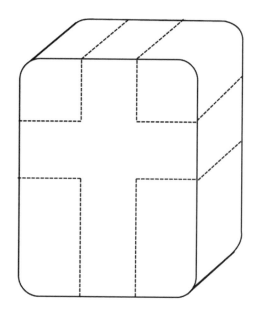

Before dinner, people of all ages are invited to make crosses that will remind them of their commitment to "take up your cross and follow me." Using table knives cut off the corners of bars of personal-sized Ivory soap (it is softer than many other bar soaps). Or, if someone in the congregation has a power saw and can pre-cut enough wooden crosses for all worshipers (about two by three inches from quarter-inch-thick wood), give each one out with a piece of very fine sandpaper and a cloth dipped in linseed oil. Early arrivers can sand and polish their crosses before dinner. Some can even polish their cross during the worship service itself.

Call to Worship

(Leader, after pancake dinner in dining room) There is a time for everything—a time for feasting, laughing, and playing in God's presence and a time for quietly thinking and praying. We have been feasting, laughing, and playing. Now it is time to be quiet, to listen, and to pray. Listen to the bells. They call us to the sanctuary to worship God. As they pass your table, get in line behind them and follow them quietly into the sanctuary for a time of worship together.

(Leader, in the sanctuary) There is a time for everything. Lent is a time for discipline. It is a time to study and pray and improve our serving. For the next six weeks until Easter we join Christians all around the world in trying to be better disciples. So come—let us listen, pray, learn, and grow.

Readings about Bearing Crosses

Readers 1 and 2 are older elementary or mid-high children. Reader 3 is an adult. All four stand close to a microphone to ensure easy hearing. In a split chancel, two readers can stand in the pulpit and two in the lectern. One good rehearsal is needed for a smooth comfortable reading.

Leader: Sometimes you hear people say, "My back hurts soooo bad. It is my cross to bear." Or, "My little brother is such a pest and my parents make me babysit him sooo much. He is a real cross to bear!" Jesus has a different idea about crosses. Jesus says two important things about crosses:

First, it isn't a cross if you don't choose it. Your aching back is not a choice. It just hurts and you have to figure out how to put up with it. You have no choice. Taking care of a little brother because your parents told you to is not a choice. It's your job in the family and you have to figure out how to do it as well as possible. Crosses can't be forced on you. You have to choose them.

Second, a cross is something you choose to do *for others*. A cross is taking risks in order to help others. If your pesky little brother is driving your dad nuts while he is trying to get some work done at home and you, without being asked, turn off your favorite TV show and get your brother to play a game with you in another room—*that*

---

is bearing a cross. You are giving up your TV show to take care of both your brother and your dad.

Jesus did his share of cross bearing before he was killed on a cross. He calls each of us to watch for and bear crosses with him. Jesus said, "Anyone who wants to be my disciple must pick up a cross and follow me." And he gave us lots of examples. Listen to stories about Jesus bearing crosses. After each story I will say, "Jesus says to us…" to which you are invited to add, "Take up a cross and follow me."

Reader 1:   Once Jesus was in a town where there was a man who was suffering from a dreaded skin disease. When he saw Jesus, he threw himself down and begged him, "Sir, if you want to, you can make me clean!" Jesus reached out and touched him. "I do want to," he answered, "Be clean!" At once the disease left the man.

Reader 3:   Why did Jesus do that! Didn't he know what a chance he took? Skin disease is very contagious. Touching a person with a skin disease could make you sick too.

Leader: Jesus says to us,

All: **"Take up your cross and follow me."**

Reader 3:   One day while Jesus and his disciples were traveling through Samaria, he sat down by a well. When a Samaritan woman came to draw water Jesus said to her, "Give me a drink of water." The woman answered, "You are a Jew and I am a Samaritan—so how can you ask me for a drink?"

Reader 2:   Good question. For one thing, Jews and Samaritans hated each other. They would not eat or drink from the same plates and cups. For another thing, men did not speak to women in public, especially women they did not know. But Jesus not only talked to a Samaritan woman, he even asked her for a cup of water.

Reader 3:   When Jesus' disciples returned and found Jesus talking with the Samaritan woman, they were greatly surprised.

Leader: Jesus says to us,

All: **"Take up your cross and follow me."**

Reader 2:   Then Levi had a big feast in his house for Jesus. There were many tax collectors at the feast. Some Pharisees and Teachers of the Law complained, "Why do you eat and drink with tax collectors and other outcasts?"

Reader 1:   Of course they complained. Tax collectors were traitors because they collected taxes for the Roman conquerors—AND—they were thieves. Most of them collected extra taxes for themselves. Good people stayed far away from them.

Reader 2: Jesus answered, "People who are well do not need a doctor, but only those who are sick. I have not come to call the respectable people to repent, but the outcasts."

Leader: Jesus says to us,

All: **"Take up your cross and follow me."**

Reader 1: Some people brought their little children to Jesus for him to place his hands on them. The disciples saw them and scolded them for bothering Jesus.

Reader 3: Jesus was an important teacher with important work do to. Whatever made parents think he had time for children?

Reader 1: But Jesus called the children to him and said, "Let the children come to me and do not stop them, because the Kingdom of God belongs to such as these. Remember this! Whoever does not receive the Kingdom of God like a child will never enter it."

Leader: Jesus says to us,

All: **"Take up your cross and follow me."**

Reader 3: After they had eaten the Last Supper, Jesus went with his disciples to the Garden of Gethsemane. He left his disciples and went apart to pray saying, "The sorrow in my heart is so great that it almost crushes me." Then, he left them to pray. He threw himself on the ground and prayed, "Father, my Father! All things are possible for you. Take this cup of suffering away from me. Still, not what I want, but what you want."

Leader: Lent is six and a half weeks before Easter when Christians try to stretch and grow. During this Lent, I challenge you to watch for crosses.
> Watch for people no one is paying any attention to.
> Watch for people who are lonely and hurting.
> Watch for people everyone else makes fun of.
Then find ways to reach out for those people—even if it costs you,
> even if your friends might laugh at you,
> even if you are not sure you can make a difference,
> even if the person you take up a cross for might not say thank you.
It is hard work. Sometimes it takes real courage. Sometimes you get hurt. Just ask Jesus. But remember:
> Jesus said bearing crosses for each other is the way we build God's Kingdom.
> Jesus also promised that every time we pick up a cross,
>> he is there with us helping out.
> And, Jesus told us a very surprising secret—
>> cross bearing can make us so happy that we do not mind the cost.
So, at least until Easter, let's try to forget ourselves and take up crosses and follow Jesus. Use your soap cross (or wood cross) as a reminder. Every time you wash your hands (or every time you see or feel your wood cross), ask yourself, "What crosses have I picked up today?" It is work of the followers of Jesus.

From *Sharing the Easter Faith with Children* by Carolyn C. Brown. © 2005 by Abingdon Press. Reproduced by permission.

Responsive Prayer

Hymn *"Lord, I Want to Be A Christian"*

I want to be more loving...
I want to be like Jesus...

Charge and Benediction

chapter five

Celebrating Palm Sunday
—or—
Looking Ahead on Passion Sunday

The Sunday before Easter presents worship planners with an important decision. Which will we celebrate—Palm Sunday or Passion Sunday? If Palm Sunday is chosen, the focus will be on Jesus' entry into Jerusalem. If Passion Sunday is chosen, the day is devoted to telling all the stories leading up to and including the crucifixion. Worship leaders must make the choice each year, considering the needs of their particular congregation in that particular year.

The decision is best based on the congregation's Holy Week calendar. If there are services that will attract worshipers of all ages for Maundy Thursday and/or Good Friday, everyone will have an opportunity to ponder the betrayal and crucifixion stories. In this case, Palm Sunday, with the focus on the entry into Jerusalem, is the choice. On the other hand, if there are no Holy Week services planned or if there are no services that will attract families with children, Passion Sunday is the better choice. Passion Sunday presents the full Holy Week story to the worshiper who will not return to the sanctuary until Easter. Without hearing the Passion story, worshipers of any age who were part of the happy Palm Sunday parade can only wonder what all the fuss over Easter is about. They need to hear the sad stories of betrayal, denial, and crucifixion. The final consideration for worship planners is the local school calendar. Many school calendars include a Spring Break around Easter time and many families with young children will be out of town for some part of Holy Week. The congregation that wants to be sure these families have a chance to hear the complete Easter story each year needs to schedule opportunities when these families will be most available to participate.

Once the decision is made, there are several ways to invite children into the celebration of either Palm or Passion Sunday.

Palm Sunday

Palm Sunday is all about the parade. The youngest preschoolers can celebrate fully with parades in their own classrooms, but older preschoolers and everyone older celebrate Palm Sunday most fully in the sanctuary. It is a day for elaborate processionals. The possibilities are limited only by our communal imagination.

Palm branch-waving children wearing either street clothes or biblical costumes can lead the choirs into the sanctuary. They may even be accompanied by a rolling donkey prop ridden by a costumed Jesus. (Occasional attempts to include a live donkey have generally proven to be a little too "over the top.") Children are old enough to participate in the processional when they have enough familiarity with the sanctuary that they will not be frightened by the big crowded room and will know how to behave. The smaller and more informal a congregation is, the younger the participants can be. Infants and toddlers can even process in carried by their parents! In larger, more formal congregations, children generally need to be at least four or five years old before joining the Palm Sunday processional.

If the weather cooperates, the entire congregation can gather outside with palm branches and process into the sanctuary together. This includes everyone and produces a reality factor of happy chaos. It also insists that Palm Sunday is not just a "cute children's thing," but a story and worship experience that is shared by Christians of all ages.

For a more formal service, choirs of all ages may do the processing with each choir member carrying a palm branch held neatly across the chest and shoulder. Older children, who are beginning to feel foolish walking around waving a palm branch spontaneously, appreciate the structure such choir processionals provide.

Neighboring congregations can merge after their individual worship services for a processional around their area with everyone waving palm branches, carrying liturgical banners or class-made posters, singing a song or two, and talking happily.

Since most Palm Sunday processionals occur at the beginning of the worship service, it is a good day to begin the Gospel storytelling with the *Call to Worship.* It is also a fine opportunity to include children in worship leadership. Here are two samples:

1. Five older elementary children take the parts of the five speakers. On cue, they run from the back of the sanctuary to the front waving their palm branches. Once at the front they turn, face the congregation and shout their parts in sequence. The rest of their classmates remain at the back of the sanctuary in two groups and shout their lines from that position. The processional hymn begins immediately following the final line. One rehearsal shortly before the service (perhaps during the church school hour) is sufficient preparation. During the rehearsal, it is necessary to work as much on getting children to really shout with enthusiasm in church as on the logistics of where to stand and what to shout. If the children's choirs are to sing, these speaking parts provide a good way to include the non-choir youngsters in the processional.

Speaker #1 *(from central aisle)*:	Jesus is coming! Jesus is coming!
Speaker #2 *(from left aisle)*:	Is he coming yet?
Speaker #3 *(from right aisle)*:	Is he really coming this way?
Group #1 *(from back left)*:	Hosanna! Hosanna!
Group #2 *(from back right)*:	Jesus is King!
Speaker #4 *(from balcony)*:	Where is he? I want to see him!
Speaker #5 *(from balcony)*:	He's coming! He's coming!
Group #1 *(from back left)*:	Hosanna! Hosanna!
Group #2 *(from back right)*:	Jesus is King!

2. For a more formal service, begin with a dialogue from Psalm 24. The older children's choirs can read the children's parts from the back of the sanctuary before processing in; or non-choir children can read the parts from the back of the sanctuary then sit as a group in reserved pews. If the worship leader is the pastor, rehearsing for this call to worship is a great opportunity to build relationships and to let the children know that they are an important part of the worshiping congregation.

Children:	Lift up your heads, O gates! and be lifted up, O ancient doors! that the King of glory may come in.
Leader:	Who is the King of glory?
Children:	The Lord, strong and mighty, the Lord, mighty in battle. Lift up your heads, O gates! and be lifted up, O ancient doors! that the King of glory may come in.
Leader:	Who is this King of glory?
Children:	The Lord of hosts, He is the King of glory.

Keep the spirit of the processional going with *a litany of Palm Sunday praise.* In response to statements describing Jesus, the congregation responds, "Hosanna!" The statements may be written by the worship leaders to fit the day's message or they may be solicited from the children and youth. A church class could create the litany as a group, working with the worship leader; or all children, youth, and adults could be invited to submit praises which a leader then knits together into one litany.

Palm Sunday is a good day to *ask a child to read the Gospel lesson.* Mark 11:1-10 is perhaps the best of the four accounts for a younger reader to read in worship.

On Palm Sunday Jesus was welcomed as God's King. Part of the task of Palm Sunday is to ponder the kind of king the crowd wanted and the kind of king Jesus came to be. *To make this visual,* display prominently a golden crown (from a party store or the Christmas pageant costumes) and a crown of thorns. During the sermon or children's message, pick each one up and talk about the kind of king who wears it. Another very visual way to explore the problem is to present the worshipers with a beautifully wrapped box. As you talk about what people expected Jesus to give them on Palm Sunday, have an elementary aged child (who is in on the secret and prepared to respond) unwrap the box before the congregation and show the congregation that it is empty. Talk with the child about how it would feel to get such a gift. Then explore how the people were disappointed that Jesus did not become the king they expected and how that set the stage for some of them to call for his death five days later.

When choosing hymns for Palm Sunday worship, choose some that children can sing. "All Glory, Laud, and Honor" with its repeated chorus is the best of the traditional Palm Sunday hymns for children. (It is especially clear when the word "laud" is introduced before the hymn is sung.) The words of "Hosanna, Loud Hosanna" are more challenging for young readers, but the children do enjoy actually singing "hosanna" and singing the storytelling verses with their emphasis on the children's participation. The language and rather subtle references to the passion of "Ride On

Ride On in Majesty" make it the hardest of the specifically Palm Sunday hymns for children to sing with understanding. If the song is familiar, children enjoy singing "Tell Me the Stories of Jesus" on the day celebrating the palm processional of verse three. "Crown Him with Many Crowns" contains no specifically Palm Sunday reference and the language of the verses is difficult for children, but with direction even the non-reader can happily join in on the repeated chorus "crown him, crown him, crown him . . ."

Passion Sunday

Passion Sunday celebrations with the long sequence of sad stories and generally somber mood are beyond the ken of preschoolers. For first and second graders, however, Passion Sunday is a good way to begin hearing the stories leading up to Jesus' death. For older elementary students, Passion Sunday is a good way to begin knitting those stories into a continuous narrative. If children are unlikely to participate in a Maundy Thursday or Good Friday service, Passion Sunday may be the only chance they have to hear the crucifixion accounts at all. So for them Passion Sunday observances planned with their participation in mind can be significant.

These children may participate with the entire congregation in a Passion Sunday service of readings and music, telling the events of Holy Week. Such services are modeled on the Christmas Lessons and Carols. Worship planners need to remember the children when selecting the texts to be read. Children have an easier time keeping up with texts that are brief and focus on the action of the week. Include children among the readers and at least some songs the children know or can sing fairly easily to further invite them into the service. In some congregations Passion Sunday may become a choir festival Sunday including choirs of all ages in telling these important stories.

It is also possible for the children to celebrate Passion Sunday very effectively with other children during either the church school or the worship hour. This may be a Holy Week "lessons and carols" service designed especially for elementary children. Or it may be a more elaborate "Walk Through Holy Week" during which the children move through the building to dramatic enactments of Holy Week scenes.

What follows is the script for a fairly elaborate "Walk Through Holy Week" in which children's classes move through Holy Week scenes scattered throughout the church building, under the leadership of a youth church school class. All the characters are costumed in biblical dress. The Production Notes that follow it suggest ways to simplify or adapt the material to fit a variety of situations.

A Journey Through Holy Week

The Palm Sunday Parade

Luke 19:28-40 (Also see Matthew 21:1-11; Mark 11:1-11; John 12:12-19)

The narrator of this scene needs to be an older youth or adult who can lead the group in the cheers with contagious enthusiasm and still keep control of the group. As the group enters, the narrator welcomes them, divides them into three groups, and rehearses each group's cheer and the whole group shouting their various cheers at once. Each group yells its line when the narrator points at it. All groups shout their lines at once when the narrator throws up both arms. When all are ready, the narrator tells the story from Luke 19:28-40 in his or her own words.

Children's Cheers

Group 1: Hosanna! Hosanna!
Group 2: Blessed is he who comes
in the name of the Lord!
Group 3: Glory to God! Glory to God!

The Story

Narrator: When Jesus went toward Jerusalem, as he neared Bethpage and Bethany on the Mount of Olives, he sent two of his disciples on ahead. He told them, "Go into the next village, where you will find a young donkey that has never been ridden. Untie the donkey and bring it here. If anyone asks why you are doing that, just say, 'The Lord needs it.' "

They went off and found everything just as Jesus had said. While they were untying the donkey, its owners asked, "Why are you doing that?"

They answered, "The Lord needs it."

Then they led the donkey to Jesus. They put some of their clothes on its back and helped Jesus get on. And as he rode along, the people spread clothes on the road in front of him. When Jesus was starting down the Mount of Olives, his large crowd of disciples were happy and praised God because of all the miracles they had seen. They shouted…

At this point the narrator points to each group in random order to yell its cheer. Like a conductor leading an orchestra, the narrator repeatedly calls on the various sections and builds the sound. Conclude with all groups shouting their cheers at once followed by an emphatic "cut" sign with arm motions. Then quietly conclude the story from Luke.

Narrator: Some Pharisees in the crowd said to Jesus, "Teacher, make your disciples stop shouting!" But Jesus answered, "If they keep quiet, these stones will start shouting."

This is where our Palm Sunday Passion Walk begins. To see what happens, next follow your guide to four days later. *(Direct group to the next setting)*

The Last Supper

John 13:1-17 (foot washing) and Matthew 26:26-30; Mark 14:22-26; Luke 22:14-20 (Last Supper)

Set a table for the Last Supper at the far end of a room. Jesus sits at the center of the table. Disciples (of both sexes) sit at the table with him. A plate of pita bread and a simple chalice sit at the middle of the table. The servant with a basin and towel stands by the door to welcome the children as they arrive and directs them to sit quietly on the floor.

Servant: *(speaking from place near the door)* Remember that back in the days of Jesus, the streets of Jerusalem were made of packed down dirt and were very dusty. Everyone wore sandals. To avoid tracking all that dirt into their homes and to give people a treat, polite hosts at a dinner party had a servant just inside the door. This servant would wash people's feet when they arrived for dinner! For the servant, it was not pleasant work! In fact, the job was given to the lowest of all the servants. But guess what happened when the disciples arrived in the room to eat dinner with Jesus . . .

Jesus did something that shocked his disciples. He took off his outer robe, tied a towel around his waist and poured water into a washbasin. They watched in amazement as he washed their feet! They were confused and amazed. Why was he doing this? When he finished washing his disciples' feet, he put his robe back on and returned to his place at the dinner table. He said:

Jesus: *(speaking from place at the table and naturally drawing the attention of the children to the other end of the room)* Do you understand what I have done to you? I, your Lord and Teacher, have just washed your feet. You should wash one another's feet. I have set an example for you, so that you will do just what I have done for you.

Disciple: *(from seat at the end of the table)* After Jesus washed our feet, we ate the Passover meal together. While we were eating, Jesus took a piece of bread, broke it, and passed it to us. "Take it," he said, "this is my body which is given for you. Eat this as a way of remembering me." Then he took a cup, gave thanks to God, and passed it to us, "This is my blood which is poured out for many for the forgiveness of sins." After dinner, we sang a song and then went out to the Garden of Gethsemane. *(Point out the door)*

Jesus may say his lines or the disciple may do all the talking with Jesus doing the motions.

Jesus Is Arrested

Matthew 26:47-56; Mark 14:43-50; Luke 22:47-53; John 18:3-11

As the group moves to their next stop, at least two soldiers step into their path and order them to sit on the hall floor. They then offer the following as if giving crisp soldiers' reports of actions carried out. Costume stores often carry inexpensive soldier kits including a sword, helmet, and shield. Scripts can be taped to the back of the shields.

Soldier 1: There was a traitor among Jesus' friends. His name was Judas. He had offered to lead us to Jesus when he was away from the crowds and easier to capture. For this information he was paid thirty silver coins.

Soldier 2: Judas led us to Jesus and his disciples in the Garden of Gethsemane. He had given us as a signal that he would kiss the one who was Jesus. We could then arrest the right man. As he stepped in front of Jesus, Jesus looked sadly at him and said, "Judas, is it with a kiss that you betray me?"

Soldier 1: When the disciples saw what was going to happen they went for their swords. One of them cut off the ear of the High Priest's slave. But, Jesus said, "Enough of this!" He touched the man's ear and healed him.

Soldier 2: Then we tied his hands and led him to the house of the High Priest. Most of the disciples disappeared, but we noticed that one, Peter, followed at a safe distance.

Soldier 1: There followed a series of so-called trials. *(Pointing to the door)* Move that way to court.

Jesus Is Tried

Matthew 26:57–27:26; Mark 14:53–15:15; Luke 22:54–23:25; John 18:12–19:16

The courtroom is set up with a small table covered with heavy, big books. A judge is seated at the table wearing a black robe. The judge presents the following as if reading from the court record.

Judge: Order in the court! Order in the court! This is what the court records say about the trial of Jesus of Nazareth:

At the High Priest's house, fake witnesses accused Jesus of saying all sorts of bad things about God. The High Priest declared that Jesus should be put to death. But since the religious leaders could not execute anyone, they took Jesus to Pilate, the Roman governor, who could order his death.

After hearing their accusations, Pilate questioned Jesus himself. He was convinced that Jesus was innocent. But he knew that the priests wanted him killed. So Pilate said nothing about Jesus' guilt or innocence. He simply asked whether the priests and the crowd with them would rather have the horrible murderer Barabbas or Jesus released. (He assumed, of course, that they would choose Jesus.) Pilate was surprised when the crowd yelled for Barabbas. Unable to save Jesus, Pilate brought out a basin of water, washed his hands in front of everyone and said, "I am not responsible for the death of this man." Then he had Jesus whipped and turned him over to them to be crucified.

Peter, who has been standing at the back of the room, walks forward and begins speaking. This is most effective if Peter speaks the story in his own words with lots of feeling.

Peter: I am Peter—one of Jesus' disciples—the one who let him down.

At dinner that night I said "Lord, I'll go with you anywhere. I am ready to die for you." I really thought I was. Jesus knew better. "Peter," he said, "before the rooster crows tomorrow morning, you will say three times that you do not even know me." I did not believe him then. But that was before everything went so wrong.

In the confusion when Jesus was arrested, I followed the crowd to the High Priest's house. There was a servant girl at the gate. She stopped me. "Aren't you one of Jesus' disciples?" she said. Scared, I said that I was not.

Because it was cold, I stood near a fire with a group of guards and servants while I waited to see what would happen to Jesus inside. One of them asked again, "Aren't you one of his disciples?" In a panic, I said, "No, I am not!" But, another man spoke up, "Didn't I see you in the garden when they arrested him?" Shaking I said, "No, I don't even know the man!" That is when I heard the rooster crow.

I remembered what Jesus said, "Before the rooster crows you will deny me three times." Some friend I turned out to be. I left the yard and wept bitterly. *(Move to the side of the room and sit facing the wall)*

Judge: *(pointing at the door)* Please move that way and follow your guide.

Jesus Is Crucified

Luke 23:32-49 (Also see Matthew 27:27-56; Mark 15:16-41; John 19:16-37)

Set the scene with a rough wooden cross at least four or five feet tall, standing upright in a bucket of rocks. Drape it with a black cloth. If possible set this scene outside. A single reader waits for the children to get in place then reads Luke 23:32-49 from an open Bible. The following is from the Contemporary English Version.

Reader: Two criminals were led out to be put to death with Jesus. When the soldiers came to the place called "The Skull," they nailed Jesus to a cross. They also nailed the two criminals to crosses, one on each side of Jesus.

Jesus said, "Father, forgive these people! They don't know what they're doing."

While the crowd stood there watching Jesus, the soldiers gambled for his clothes. The leaders insulted him by saying, "He saved others. Now he should save himself, if he really is God's chosen Messiah!"

The soldiers made fun of Jesus and brought him some wine. They said, "If you are the king of the Jews, save yourself!"

Above him was a sign that said, "This is the King of the Jews."

One of the criminals hanging there also insulted Jesus by saying, "Aren't you the Messiah? Save yourself and save us!"

But the other criminal told the first one off, "Don't you fear God? Aren't you getting the same punishment as this man? We got what was coming to us, but he didn't do anything wrong." Then he said to Jesus, "Remember me when you come into power!"

Jesus replied, "I promise that today you will be with me in paradise."

Around noon the sky turned dark and stayed that way until the middle of the afternoon. The sun stopped shining, and the curtain in the temple split down the middle. Jesus shouted, "Father, I put myself in your hands!" Then he died.

When the Roman officer saw what had happened, he praised God and said, "Jesus must really have been a good man!"

A crowd had gathered to see the terrible sight. Then after they had seen it, they felt brokenhearted and went home. All of Jesus' close friends and the women who had come with him from Galilee stood at a distance and watched.

Close the Bible and instruct the children to quietly follow their guide.

From *Sharing the Easter Faith with Children* by Carolyn C. Brown. © 2005 by Abingdon Press. Reproduced by permission.

Jesus Is Buried

Luke 23:50-56 (Also see Matthew 27:57-61; Mark 15:42-47; John 19:38-42)

If there is a cemetery, memorial garden, columbarium, or any other spot the children will connect with people who have died, go to that place for the final stop. If there is no such spot, select a garden or quiet indoor space. A single reader wearing a white robe and gold sash tied over one shoulder presents the following, from Luke 23:50-56 (CEV). It is most effective if the reader knows it well enough to present it in his or her own words "by heart."

Reader: There was a man named Joseph from Arimathea, a good and honorable man. He asked Pontius Pilate for the body of Jesus. Then he took the body down, wrapped it in a linen sheet, and placed it in a tomb which had been dug out of solid rock and which had never been used. It was Friday and the Sabbath was about to begin.

The women who had followed Jesus from Galilee went with Joseph and saw the tomb and how Jesus' body was placed in it. Then they went back home and prepared the spices and perfumes for the body.

On the Sabbath they rested, as the Law commanded.

Very early on Sunday morning the women went to the tomb, carrying the spices they had prepared…

(Pause briefly)

That is where we leave the story now. We all know that there is another step, an exciting, happy step on this path—one that will have to wait until next Sunday, 'til Easter. This week is a time to remember the story and to wait.

At this point mention any ways your congregation offers for children to remember Holy Week. Note worship services appropriate for children and any calendars or devotional books available for their use at home. Conclude with mention of Easter morning plans and instructions to return to their classrooms with their guides.

Production Notes

1. This Walk was written to be produced by teenagers for elementary schoolers. The teenagers delve more deeply into the Holy Week stories as they prepare the scenes for presentation to the younger children. The younger children listen more attentively to the stories because they are presented by the teenagers rather than by adults. Preparations take up several weeks of youth church school classes. The first year or two this production was done, there was no script. The youth were challenged to read the texts and "put the stories into their own words." The results were very uneven. Those who took their task seriously delivered absolutely stunning performances that spoke powerfully to both the children and their adult teachers. But a significant number gave it little thought and therefore gave poor performances, even sharing inaccurate information. A few failed to show up on Passion Sunday. These experiences led the adults to produce scripts that the youth could use verbatim or as a starting point for their own presentation of their assigned character and story. The younger the youth, the more likely they are to depend on the printed script.

2. When teenagers sponsor this Walk, it requires lots of adult support. Particularly when younger teens are the actors, there needs to be a knowledgeable adult at each scene to prompt beginnings and endings and to help respond to surprises. Each group of traveling children is also well served by an adult guide who moves with them, helps them participate at each stop, and is available to answer questions between stops. Their church school teachers are obvious guides. Give the teachers full information about the plan for the Walk and its goals to help them keep things moving and interpret what is going on for their children.

3. This script has children move through a series of church school rooms and other spots around the church campus. The movement emphasizes the fact that these stories took place over several days in several places scattered around the city of Jerusalem. If space is limited or moving around is difficult, the entire "Journey" could take place in one large room. In this case the scenes could be set up around the perimeter with the children seated in the middle. Or the scenes could be a series of dramatic readings presented from the same spot at the front of a room. This latter approach can be more like a Passion Sunday service of lessons and carols designed especially for children.

4. Think ahead about how many children will be in how much space. Also think about acoustics. It is possible to send the children on the Journey in two waves with the second wave starting just after the first clears the Palm Sunday scene. During a church school hour, the first and second graders, who tend to move more slowly, could go in one group, followed by the third through fifth graders. More than two waves cannot make the trip in a one-hour period. No matter what the size of the room, keep the number of participants in it at any one time to fewer than forty, if microphones are not used. For outside scenes, keep the children close to the speaker and when possible stand the speaker in front of a wall that will bounce the sound toward the listeners.

5. This script is meant to be a guide. It can be adapted to fit different congregations and from year to year, to keep it lively in the same congregation. For example, consider replacing a dramatic scene with a few minutes of a commercial video presenting one of the stories. Also note that no music is suggested. Singing familiar Holy Week songs at appropriate scenes would certainly add to the experience. All the children could sing in response to the telling of a story, or some of the youth could sing as part of their presentation. Instrumentalists could provide background music as children come and go from a room, e.g., a drummer with the soldiers or at the cross.

Create a Holy Week Devotional Book on Passion Sunday

Another way to celebrate Passion Sunday with children during the church school hour is to review the Holy Week stories and to prepare children for a week of rereading the stories at home. In the process, children who are not likely to hear the Passion stories elsewhere will hear them at least once. Children are also challenged to celebrate Holy Week on their own by using a devotional book that they have assembled. This is especially effective with third- through fifth-graders who can read on their own; it can also be effective with first- and second-graders, if their families are alerted to the project and encouraged to make each day's readings a family discipline for Holy Week. The pages at the end of this chapter form the body of the book.

Before class: Adults copy the pages of the devotional book onto stiff paper, gather the props that the children will add to each page, fold purple 12" x 18" sheets of construction paper in half for covers, and be sure hole punches and yarn are available to secure the pages into "books."

During class: Students hear or read each of the stories for the week and add a symbol to each page of their book (see the table on the following page). This may involve simply reading the stories printed in the devotional book or it may include presenting each story in a different way. For example, view a section of a video, read directly from the Bible, or read a storybook version of a story from the church library. In either case the goal is the same—to present the Passion stories in a meaningful way to the children.

To assemble the book, children tie yarn or ribbon through each hole separately forming two or three rings in each book rather than thread yarn through two holes forming a single loop in each book. This makes the book with all its attachments easier to use and more likely to last the week.

Students may work through the days of the week as a class or may rotate in small groups through a series of centers at which they encounter the stories and gather the symbols. A single class could do this independently or several classes could work together on the project.

Adaptations

1. These pages print out the texts for the benefit of children (or parents) who may have difficulty finding the texts in a Bible. The aim is to make the daily readings as easy as possible. If you think your children and their families can easily find the texts, replace the printed stories with the biblical references. This builds reader comfort with reading the Bible.

2. Rather than make the book with all its attachments, you could simply provide students with a bookmark listing the biblical texts to read from their Bibles during the week.

3. The devotional book can be adapted to match the stops of a "Journey Through Holy Week" with children collecting the symbols at each stop along the journey. This requires that the pages be prepared and easy to pass to the children as they file out of a room.

Symbols to Add to the Pages of the Devotional Book

Palm Sunday:	Tape or staple a palm leaf to this page. Children might use it for a bookmark during the week.
Monday:	Glue a small bird feather to the page. (Bags of feathers are available in craft stores.)
Tuesday:	Tape several play money coins onto this page.
Wednesday:	Glue a crystal teardrop on this page. (Crystal teardrops with flat backs are available in the bead section of craft stores.) The children draw the heart around it as they use the book during the week.
Maundy Thursday:	Pre-pack several pieces of matzo (available at most grocery stores) in a plastic bag for each book. Clip or staple the bags to this page.
Good Friday:	Tape a nail to the page to hold while reading the crucifixion story.
Saturday:	Add nothing for this day of waiting
Easter Sunday:	Add Easter stickers that say "He is Risen!" or "Alleluia!"

A Journey Through Holy Week

Palm Sunday

Read about the Palm Sunday parade led by Jesus and his disciples.

When they were getting close to Jerusalem, Jesus sent two disciples on ahead. He told them, "Go into the next village. As soon as you enter it, you will find a young donkey that has never been ridden. Untie the donkey and bring it here. If anyone asks why you are doing that, say, 'The Lord needs it and will soon bring it back.' "

The disciples left and found the donkey tied near a door that faced the street. While they were untying it, some of the people standing there asked, "Why are you untying the donkey?" They told them what Jesus had said, and the people let them take it.

The disciples led the donkey to Jesus. They put some of their clothes on its back, and Jesus got on. Many people spread clothes on the road, while others went to cut branches from the fields.

In front of Jesus and behind him, people went along shouting, "Hosanna! God bless the one who comes in the name of the Lord!"

Make up your own Hosanna prayer-poem for God. In the space below, write a prayer that begins with each letter in the word Hosanna.

H _____

O _____

S _____

A _____

N _____

N _____

A _____

Pray your Hosanna prayer for God!

Scripture Note: Mark 11:1-9 (CEV); "Hooray" changed to "Hosanna"; "them" in first paragraph changed to "two disciples."

Jesus went back to the Temple. Read about what he did.

When they arrived in Jerusalem, Jesus went to the Temple and began to drive out all those who were buying and selling. He overturned the tables of the moneychangers and the stools of those who sold pigeons, and he would not let anyone carry anything through the Temple court-yards. He then taught the people: "It is written in the Scriptures that God said, 'My Temple will be called a house of prayer for the people of all nations.' But you have turned it into a hideout for thieves!"

The chief priests and the teachers of the Law heard of this, so they began looking for some way to kill Jesus. They were afraid of him, because the whole crowd was amazed at his teaching.

The Jerusalem Journal

MONDAY EDITION

If you were a reporter sent to cover this story, you would ask these questions. Can you answer them all?

❏ What did Jesus do at the Temple?

❏ Why did he do that?

❏ How did the Temple leaders feel about what Jesus did and said?

Glue
Feather
Here

Scripture Note: Mark 11:15-18 (GNT)

Tuesday

Read the sad story about what Judas did during Holy Week.

Judas Iscariot was one of the twelve disciples. He went to the chief priests and asked, "How much will you give me if I help you arrest Jesus?" They paid Judas thirty silver coins, and from then on he started looking for a good chance to betray Jesus.

On Thursday night after dinner, Judas led a mob sent by the leaders to Jesus and his disciples in the Garden of Gethsemane. Judas had told them ahead of time, "Arrest the man I greet with a kiss."

Judas walked right up to Jesus and said, "Hello, teacher." Then Judas kissed him.

The men grabbed Jesus and arrested him. One of Jesus' followers pulled out a sword. He struck the servant of the high priest and cut off his ear.

But Jesus told him, "Put your sword away. Anyone who lives by fighting will die by fighting." All of Jesus' disciples left him and ran away.

When Judas learned that Jesus had been sentenced to death, he was sorry for what he had done. He returned the thirty silver coins to the chief priests and leaders and said, "I have sinned by betraying a man who has never done anything wrong."

"So what? That's your problem," they replied. Judas threw the money into the Temple and then went out and hanged himself.

Tape Coins Here

Scripture Note: Selected verses from Matthew 26:14-25, 47-50, and 27:3-5 (CEV); second paragraph is author's summary of Matthew 26:26-46; "he" changed to "Judas" in text from Matthew 27:3.

Wednesday

Peter was one of Jesus' very best friends. He had lived and worked and played with Jesus for three years. He loved Jesus and knew that Jesus came from God. But he got frightened. Read what Peter did.

During dinner Thursday night, Peter said, "Lord, I am ready to go with you to jail and even to die with you."

Jesus replied, "Peter, I tell you that before a rooster crows tomorrow morning, you will say three times that you don't know me."

Later that same night Jesus was arrested and led away to the house of the high priest, while Peter followed at a distance. Some people built a fire in the middle of the courtyard and were sitting around it. Peter sat there with them, and a servant girl saw him. Then after she had looked at him carefully, she said, "This man was with Jesus!"

Peter said, "Woman, I don't even know that man!"

A little later someone else saw Peter and said, "You are one of them!"

"No, I'm not!" Peter replied.

About an hour later another man insisted, "This man must have been with Jesus. They both come from Galilee."

Peter replied, "I don't know what you are talking about!" Right then, while Peter was still speaking, a rooster crowed.

The Lord turned and looked at Peter. And Peter remembered that the Lord had said, "Before a rooster crows tomorrow morning, you will say three times that you don't know me." Then Peter went out and cried hard.

Find the happy ending to this story in John 21:1-19. Then draw a heart around the teardrop at the top of this page because Jesus forgives Peter and us.

Scripture Note: Luke 22:31-34, 54-62 (CEV); "During dinner Thursday night" and "Later that same night" added for sense of timing.

From *Sharing the Easter Faith with Children* by Carolyn C. Brown. © 2005 by Abingdon Press. Reproduced by permission.

Maundy Thursday

Today we remember Jesus' last meal with his disciples before he was killed. It was also the night he invented communion. At one meal today, put the package of matzo and this book in the middle of your table. Read the story aloud while everyone at the table eats a piece of matzo.

The day came during the Festival of Unleavened Bread when the lambs for the Passover meal were to be killed. Jesus sent off Peter and John with these instructions: "Go and get the Passover meal ready for us to eat."

"Where do you want us to get it ready?" they asked him.

He answered, "As you go into the city, a man carrying a jar of water will meet you. Follow him into the house that he enters, and say to the owner of the house: 'The Teacher says to you, Where is the room where my disciples and I will eat the Passover meal?' He will show you a large furnished room upstairs, where you will get everything ready."

They went off and found everything just as Jesus had told them, and they prepared the Passover meal.

When the hour came, Jesus took his place at the table with the apostles. He said to them, "I have wanted so much to eat this Passover meal with you before I suffer! For I tell you, I will never eat it until it is given its full meaning in the Kingdom of God."

Then Jesus took a cup, gave thanks to God, and said, "Take this and share it among yourselves. I tell you that from now on I will not drink this wine until the Kingdom of God comes."

Then he took a piece of bread, gave thanks to God, broke it, and gave it to them, saying, "This is my body, which is given for you. Do this in memory of me." In the same way, he gave them the cup after the supper, saying, "This cup is God's new covenant sealed with my blood, which is poured out for you."

Scripture Note: Luke 22:7-20 (GNT)

Good Friday

Read this story about Good Friday.

After Pilate ruled that Jesus be whipped and crucified, soldiers took Jesus to a hill outside of town. They drove big nails through the bones in his wrists and into a long wooden beam. Then they lifted the beam into place at the top of a pole leaving Jesus hanging by the nails. They drove one more nail through his feet and into the pole, and placed a sign over Jesus' head. The sign said, "Jesus of Nazareth, King of the Jews." By then it was nine o'clock in the morning.

People from town made fun of Jesus, "You say you are God's King. Let's see you save yourself now!" The soldiers rolled dice for his clothes while they waited for him to die. But Jesus looked down from the cross and said, "Father, forgive them. They do not know what they are doing."

Two robbers were crucified with Jesus. One joined the crowd yelling at Jesus, "If you are God's Son, save yourself and save us, too!" But the other robber said, "Be quiet! We are getting what we deserve. Jesus is innocent." Then he whispered to Jesus, "Remember me when you come as God's King." Jesus quietly replied, "I promise that you will be with me today in paradise."

When Jesus saw his mother watching with his friend John, he said to John, "Take care of her as if she were your mother." And he said to his mother, "John will be like a son to you now."

In the middle of the day, the sky turned darkest black. Jesus spoke to God, "Into your hands I give my spirit" and died. The captain of the soldiers looked up at Jesus and said, "This man really was God's Son."

That same day, Joseph of Arimathea bravely asked Pilate for permission to bury Jesus' body. He took it down from the cross, wrapped it in a long linen sheet, and laid it on a ledge in a new cave tomb. After the women, who had stayed with Jesus until he died, saw where Jesus' body was laid, they went home broken-hearted and exhausted.

Tape Nail Here

Saturday

Saturday was a sad, quiet day for Jesus' friends. They could not believe Jesus was dead.

Saturday of Holy Week is a quiet day for Christians today. We remember all the sad stories of Holy Week and quietly get ready for the happy Sunday that is coming.

To get ready for Easter write an Easter prayer for tomorrow. Think back over the stops on our Holy Week journey then finish each of the prayer sentences below.

Thank you, God, for _____

_____

We're sorry, God, about _____

_____

God, help us _____

_____

We pray in Jesus' name. Amen.

Easter Sunday
Christ is Risen! Happy Easter! Alleluia!

Easter is the happiest day in the year for Christians. Read Matthew's story about what happened on the first Easter.

After the Sabbath, as Sunday morning was dawning, Mary Magdalene and the other Mary went to look at the tomb. Suddenly there was a violent earthquake; an angel of the Lord came down from heaven, rolled the stone away, and sat on it. His appearance was like lightning, and his clothes were white as snow. The guards were so afraid that they trembled and became like dead men.

The angel spoke to the women. "You must not be afraid," he said. "I know you are looking for Jesus, who was crucified. He is not here; he has been raised, just as he said. Come here and see the place where he was lying. Go quickly now, and tell his disciples, 'He has been raised from death, and now he is going to Galilee ahead of you; there you will see him!' Remember what I have told you."

So they left the tomb in a hurry, afraid and yet filled with joy, and ran to tell his disciples.

Alleluia! Alleluia! Alleluia! Alleluia! Alleluia!

Collect "Alleluias" today. The word "Alleluia" is not in the Bible story about Easter but if you stay alert you may see, hear, say, and sing it lots today. You might see an "Alleluia!" in a banner or on a poster. You may hear a choir sing the word. You will almost certainly sing an Easter song with over a dozen "Alleluias" in it! Listen for "Alleluia!" in prayers too. "Alleluia!" means praise and thank God.

Alleluia! Alleluia! Alleluia! Alleluia! Alleluia!

Scripture Note: Matthew 28:1-8 (GNT)

chapter six

Maundy Thursday: Recalling the Last Supper

Maundy Thursday worship can be a very important experience for elementary children. Just as the story of Jesus' birth has more power on Christmas Eve, the story of the Last Supper has more power on Maundy Thursday. "On this very night, years ago in Jerusalem, the night before he was killed, Jesus…" Young imaginations try to put themselves in the Upper Room to hear, see, taste, and smell what happened. Maundy Thursday may also be the best or only opportunity the church has to speak of the Passion to children and their families in worship. Congregations do well to encourage children and their families to attend Maundy Thursday worship. Larger congregations may create a service especially for children and their families. Most congregations, however, can plan Maundy Thursday services that intentionally include worshipers of all ages.

Whether the service is planned especially for families or for the entire congregation with children present, three facets of the night influence the service. First of all, it celebrates two meals, the Last Supper and Holy Communion. Eating and drinking together is the centerpiece. Second, the Last Supper was not just any meal, but a Passover Meal. Older elementary children are ready to learn about the Passover and its connection to Communion. And third, Maundy Thursday always looks forward to Good Friday. Even if Good Friday worship provides an opportunity to ponder the Passion, Communion on Thursday interprets the events of Friday. So it is important to think about how the Passion will figure in Maundy Thursday celebrations that include children. This chapter considers these facets in order.

The Meals

The Last Supper takes place at a dinner table. It is this meal at a table that interprets the Communion meal the church celebrates in the sanctuary throughout the year. Worship that dramatizes and connects these meals helps children both place themselves in the Upper Room on Maundy Thursday and participate more fully in every celebration of the sacrament. To focus on the meals, Maundy Thursday worship may take place not in the sanctuary, but in the room where the church generally serves meals. It may actually begin with a meal. Or, though worshipers are seated around tables as if eating, Communion may be the only meal served. The service could also be held in the sanctuary with special efforts made to highlight the dinner table aspect of Communion.

If worship begins with a meal, long tables are set up to form a large cross in the middle of the room with additional tables set in rows at the foot of the cross or as a border around the central table. Because it is a special night, the meal should be different from ordinary church suppers. Set the tables with cloth tablecloths, china plates, stainless rather than plastic cutlery, and candles. Serve a "Sunday dinner" type meal. Encourage families to sit as families if that is not the norm for other church meals. All this effort tells children that this is not just any other church supper. It is indeed a special night.

Telling the Last Supper story permeates the whole meal. It begins with the story of Jesus' washing the disciples' feet. The presenter of the story enters the room costumed in a simple biblical tunic with a towel over his shoulder and tells the story in his own words as he walks forward. He may or may not actually wash someone's feet. Or the presenter simply stands in street clothes in his place at a table to read the story directly from the scripture. The worship leader follows the story with words of welcome and the invitation to diners to hold hands for a mealtime blessing.

At intervals during the meal, other stories from the Gospel accounts of the Last Supper are read. Announce each reading by ringing a bell or flicking the lights to draw attention and interrupt table conversations. Judas' departure (Matthew 26:20-25) and the new commandment (John 13:34) are the most important stories to children. Short sections from the monologues in John's version can also be added. The final story is the institution of the sacrament and occurs as soon as diners have finished their meals. After a reader reads the biblical text, the worship leader speaks from the head of the tables pointing out that just as Jesus offered his friends bread and wine at the end of their meal that night, she or he offers all worshipers bread and wine in Jesus' name at the end of this meal on this night. Serving is done around the tables. Following the sacrament, worshipers sing a song together and leave.

During this service and most other Maundy Thursday services, match the serving of the sacrament to the story by using intinction, wherein worshipers dip pieces of bread into a chalice of wine. If they are seated at tables, worshipers can easily pass the elements among themselves. At smaller services a single chalice can be passed all the way around the table. At larger services, each table needs its own loaf and chalice. Sliding the elements along the table allows children to handle the bread trays and chalice with minimum threat of spills.

If the service is conducted around tables without serving a meal, arrange tables in the cross format described above and set with candles, bread and chalice, and printed orders of worship. Invite worshipers to enter talking informally. The service begins with the lighting of the candles at all the tables during announced silence or musical prelude. Readers stand to read at different places around the tables. In this case the service is structured as a meal and printed bulletins at each place use meal vocabulary (as in the following example).

An Order of Worship for
Maundy Thursday Worship Around Tables

The Invitation

Reader: Mark 14:12-16 (Preparations for the Last Supper)
Worship Leader welcomes all and introduces the service.

Song

"I Come With Joy"

The Welcome

Reader: John 13:4-17 (Jesus washes the disciples' feet)
Worship Leader offers either meditation or prayers for each other and the world.

A Diner Departs Early

Reader: Matthew 26:20-25 (Judas' departure)
Worship Leader leads prayers of confession.

Table Conversation

Reader: John 13:34 (A new commandment)
Worship Leader offers either a meditation or leads responsive prayers of intercession to
which the congregation responds, "Teach us to love one another."

The Main Course

Reader: Mark 14:22-25
Celebration of the Sacrament

Song

"For the Bread Which You Have Broken"

Benediction

If the service is held in the sanctuary, it will probably follow the standard order of worship. Within that order, dramatize the meal by actually setting the Communion table during the service. Begin the celebration of Communion with a small procession. Two people carry in the tablecloth and spread it on the Communion table, taking time to be sure it is straight and flat. Their care illustrates the importance of the meal to be served there. They are followed by people, including some children, who carry the trays of bread and chalice, which they place in the appropriate places on the table. (A rehearsal is definitely required to do this smoothly.) To increase the involvement of the children and emphasize the fact that this is a feast prepared by and for the family, ask a children's class to bake the bread and pour the wine into the chalices for this service.

Another way (one beyond worship) to enrich the congregation's understanding of the meal is to collect Last Supper art in the same way many congregations collect Christmas crèches. People have been drawing, painting, sculpting, and weaving renditions of the Last Supper for centuries. Each artist has something to say about the Last Supper. When Italian Leonardo da Vinci painted his famous version of the Last Supper, he put a big window in the background. Through the window he painted not the skyline of Jerusalem, but an Italian countryside. He wanted people to consider the possibility that the fellowship of the Last Supper was not long ago and far away, but could happen now. Many current artists paint women and children as well as men into their pictures. You may find the beginnings of such a collection among old church school picture files in a storage closet. Another source is the gift shops and catalogs of art museums. Look for old works and contemporary works from around the world. As the congregation becomes familiar with the collection, members will watch for new additions to suggest.

Pieces of the collection may be used to illustrate sermons or class lessons throughout the year. The entire collection can be prominently displayed each year during Lent. Position items so that children as well as adults can view them. To encourage viewers to "see" the art and think about what it says about the Last Supper, post descriptive materials and open ended questions by each work. For example, by da Vinci's painting, "Look out the window. The artist painted, not Jerusalem, but an Italian scene most viewers would see every day. He wanted to make them think about meeting Jesus everyday. What scene might da Vinci have put in his window today?" Children's grade school classes may visit the display and respond by creating their own art works.

The Passover Connection

The meal Jesus and his disciples ate together that night was the Passover feast. Thoughtful theologians, beginning with the New Testament writers, have dwelt on the parallels between the Exodus and Jesus' Passion and Resurrection. Older elementary children, especially those with Jewish friends or relatives, are fascinated by this intersection of the faiths. But understanding the connection requires more detailed knowledge of both the Exodus/Passover and the Passion/Resurrection narratives than we can assume for most of today's children or their parents. It is also too much to explain during Maundy Thursday worship when so much else is going on. Church school classes and congregational events offer better opportunities to dig into this material.

]Elementary students need to read the Old Testament and New Testament stories side by side. The biblical Passover story is fairly long and complicated with many significant details. Even the biblical summary in Exodus 12:21-28 must be set in context by the teacher or storyteller. Given this, it is often helpful to turn to Bible storybooks for condensed versions. After reviewing the Passover story and reading one of the gospel accounts of the Last Supper, children can identify how bread is used in both. The Passover bread recalls the unleavened bread carried out of Egypt while the Last Supper bread reminds us of Jesus' body broken for us. Only the oldest children can begin exploring what it means to call Jesus the "Passover Lamb" or "Lamb of God." Passover lambs were real lambs whose blood was a signal to God to pass over that house. Jesus is not a lamb but a person. He is called the Lamb of God because, just as the death of the Passover lambs signaled freedom from slavery, Jesus' death signaled freedom from sin (forgiveness). To avoid the problems atonement theology poses for children, it is best to treat "Lamb of God" as a sacred nickname for Jesus.

One of the richest ways to teach worshipers of all ages about the connection between Passover and the Last Supper is to invite a rabbi or other Jewish leader to walk families through a Passover seder. This congregational event might begin with a meal featuring traditional Jewish Passover foods. A Passover table is set up as a "stage set" from which the guest can speak. Or the leader prepares a Passover plate to illustrate the ritual. An older elementary church school class can invite a Jewish adult or family to walk them through Passover in their classroom. This is especially effective if the children already know the person or family—perhaps the family of a friend or a teacher or coach many of the children know. While participants at the congregational event can count on the Jewish leader to tell them the biblical story, it is often best for children to hear and study that story before receiving a guest in their classroom. Participants in both types of events also benefit by follow-up conversations about how Christians connect Passover and Holy Communion. Interfaith respect dictates that these conversations take place after the Jewish guests have departed. A second event (maybe the next in a series of Lenten meals) or the next Sunday's sermon can focus on the Christian interpretation of Passover. Classroom activities focused on the Last Supper's Passover connection can be planned for the Sunday following the visit of the Jewish guest. The knowledge participants gather from this exposure to the Jewish celebration of Passover enriches their participation in Communion on Maundy Thursday and on other days of the years.

When members of the congregation have at least a minimal understanding of Passover, worship planners can include elements of Passover in Maundy Thursday worship. For example, the sermon can be structured as a series of questions and answers. Just as a child asks a series of questions about the meaning of Passover during the feast, the sermon might be set up as a series of questions posed by a child with answers offered by the preacher. Possible questions to explore include but are not limited to the following:

- Why is this night different from all other nights? (the first Passover question)
- Why do we eat bread to remember Jesus?
- Why this kind of bread? (wafer, matzo, loaf)
- Why do we drink grape juice or wine to remember Jesus?
- Why do we eat only these little bits of bread and drink tiny sips of wine?
- What does it mean for us to eat this bread and drink from this cup?

While the Passover connection enriches the Christian celebration of the Last Supper, understanding it is not necessary for meaningful participation in Maundy Thursday worship. Especially with children, the starting point on Maundy Thursday is the Christian celebration. Add the Passover connections only to enrich what they already know and value about Jesus' institution of Holy Communion.

Looking Ahead to the Passion on Maundy Thursday

The Last Supper is the first scene in the Passion narrative. It interprets all the scenes that follow. So, on Maundy Thursday, we come to the table already thinking ahead to the cross. Since many worshipers will not worship on Good Friday and may have only limited familiarity with the details of the biblical stories around the cross, Maundy Thursday is a good night for storytelling.

Sermons that draw on stories rather than ideas can have great impact. Jesus said, "Do this to remember me." Use the sermon to remember stories about Jesus with emphasis on the Passion stories.

Tell your favorite stories about Jesus and tell why you like them. Invite listeners to remember their favorite stories. Conclude by remembering the most important and difficult stories, those around the cross. Or select one person who was present at the Last Supper; follow Peter, Thomas, Phillip, even Judas through the crucifixion and resurrection. See what happened through their eyes and reflect on their experiences. In the process you invite listeners of all ages to imagine what might have happened to them had they witnessed the Passion.

One of the most impressive ways to tell the Passion story is **Tenebrae**. Tenebrae is most appropriately a Good Friday ritual, but is often celebrated after Communion on Maundy Thursday. It is a candle lighting service in reverse, beginning with all candles lit. As each section of the passion is read, a candle is snuffed until after the final reading about Jesus' death, the room is dark. A single candle is relit signifying the hope of the resurrection and worshipers leave in silence.

Readers may be seated at a long table with a candle at each place. In this case, the readings begin at the ends and work toward the middle with the central candle being the last one snuffed and the one relit. (Two snuffers with one starting at each end of the table are essential.)

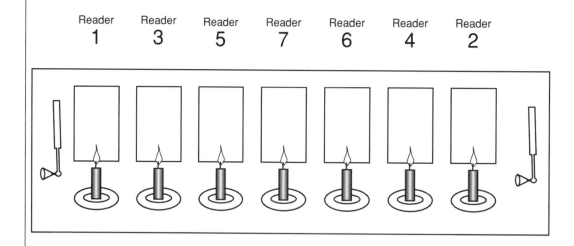

Reader 1	Reader 3	Reader 5	Reader 7	Reader 6	Reader 4	Reader 2

Readers may come to the lectern from seats nearby to read. In this case, an acolyte snuffs out candles on a central candelabrum after each reading. As always with services of readings, children appreciate having children included among the readers. To be effective, Tenebrae requires one nighttime rehearsal at which lighting issues as well as reading issues can be addressed. A plan is needed for slowly turning out the sanctuary lights in tandem with snuffing the candles. The growing darkness makes this a powerful ritual. It is most effective for children if the readings are not too long and focus on the action of the story.

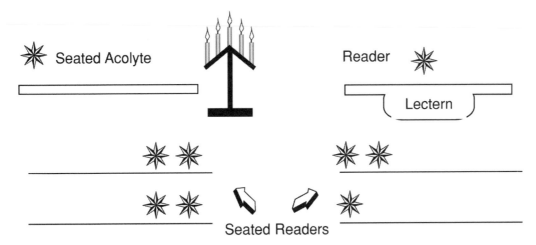

Readers may come to the lectern from seats nearby to read. In this case, an acolyte

A sample script follows. Match the readings to the reader. The final reading, "Jesus Is Buried" can be easily read by a second grader who is a good reader and will read in a clear voice. Adults who are also good readers are needed for some of the longer more complicated stories. When possible, choose readers who are recognized by children as well as adults. When children hear a well-liked coach or church school teacher read a story, they listen, assuming that it is important to the reader and therefore might be important to them also. Help all the readers by providing scripts with which to practice at home and large-print versions for reading during the service.

Obviously, there are choices to be made. Though all three concerns (the meals, Passover, and looking to Passion) may shape each year, all three cannot be the focus every year. That provides opportunity for variety in celebrating this important night and story.

Tenebrae Readings

The texts for the readings below are taken from or based on the Contemporary English Version (CEV), the Good News Translation (GNT), and the New Revised Standard Version (NRSV). They were chosen and shaped with the presence of elementary children in mind.

The Last Supper

While they were eating, Jesus took a loaf of bread, and after blessing it he broke it, gave it to the disciples, and said, "Take, eat; this is my body." Then he took a cup, and after giving thanks he gave it to them, saying, "Drink from it, all of you; for this is my blood,…which is poured out for many for the forgiveness of sins. I tell you, I will never again drink of the fruit of the vine until that day when I drink it new with you in my Father's kingdom."

When they had sung the hymn, they went out to the Mount of Olives.

—Matthew 26:26-30 (NRSV)

Jesus Prays in a Garden

They came to a place called Gethsemane, and Jesus said to his disciples, "Sit here while I pray." He took Peter, James, and John with him. Distress and anguish came over him, and he said to them, "The sorrow in my heart is so great that it almost crushes me. Stay here and keep watch."

He went a little farther on, threw himself on the ground, and prayed that, if possible, he might not have to go through that time of suffering. "Father," he prayed, "my Father! All things are possible for you. Take this cup of suffering away from me. Yet not what I want, but what you want."

Then he returned and found the three disciples asleep. He said to Peter, "Simon, are you asleep? Weren't you able to stay awake even for one hour?" And he said to them, "Keep watch, and pray that you will not fall into temptation. The spirit is willing, but the flesh is weak."

He went away once more and prayed, saying the same words. Then he came back to the disciples and found them asleep; they could not keep their eyes open. And they did not know what to say to him.

When he came back the third time, he said to them, "Are you still sleeping and resting? Enough! The hour has come! Look, the Son of Man is now being handed over to the power of sinners. Get up, let us go. Look, here is the man who is betraying me!"

—Mark 14:32-42 (GNT)

Jesus Is Arrested

Jesus was still speaking when Judas, one of the twelve disciples, arrived. With him was a crowd armed with swords and clubs and sent by the chief priests, the teachers of the Law, and the elders. The traitor had given the crowd a signal: "The man I kiss is the one you want. Arrest him and take him away under guard."

As soon as Judas arrived, he went up to Jesus and said, "Teacher!" and kissed him. So they arrested Jesus and held him tight.

—Mark 14:43-46 (GNT)

Peter Denies Even Knowing Jesus

Simon Peter followed Jesus staying by the gate to the building where they took Jesus. A girl at the gate said to Peter, "Aren't you also one of the disciples of that man?"

"No, I am not," answered Peter.

It was cold, so the servants and guards had built a charcoal fire and were standing round it, warming themselves. Peter went over and stood with them.

One of the guards said to him, "Aren't you also one of the disciples of that man?"

But Peter denied it. "No, I am not," he said.

Then a slave of the High Priest spoke up. "Didn't I see you with him in the garden?"

Again Peter said "No!"

At that moment a cock crowed, and Peter remembered what Jesus had told him: "Before the cock crows, you will say three times that you do not know me." He went out and wept bitterly.

—Based on Matthew 26:69-75; John 18:15-18, 25-27 (NRSV)

Jesus Is Tried

The soldiers first took Jesus to the High Priest's house where the religious leaders held a trial. After many witnesses spoke, but did not agree with each other, the High Priest turned to Jesus and asked, "Is it true that you are the Messiah, the Son of God?" Jesus answered, "So you say." Angrily the High Priest tore his robe and yelled, "Blasphemy! You have heard what he said. We need no more witnesses. He deserves to die!"

Because they did not have the power to execute a person, the religious leaders took Jesus to Pilate, the Roman governor. After questioning Jesus, Pilate decided that he did not deserve to die. Because he wanted to save Jesus, he offered the crowd a choice. "Every year at Passover," he said, "I release one prisoner. This year I can release Barabbas, the murderer, or Jesus. Which would you prefer?" He made this offer because he was sure they would choose Jesus. But he was wrong. At the urging of their leaders, the crowd shouted for Barabbas. Pilate was surprised. "What then shall I do with Jesus?" he asked. "Crucify him!" they yelled. "Crucify him! Crucify him!" They yelled over and over.

Pilate shrugged. He called for a bowl of water and a towel and washed his hands in front of the whole crowd. "I am not responsible for this man's death," he said as he dried his hands with the towel. Then he gave orders for Barabbas to be released and for Jesus to be whipped and crucified.

The soldiers took Jesus to their barracks. They put a royal robe on him and mashed a crown of thorns onto his head. They bowed before him and taunted him, "Hail, King of the Jews!" When they grew tired of this game, they led him out to be executed.

—Based on Matthew 26:57-67; 27:11-31 (NRSV)

Jesus Is Killed

The soldiers took Jesus to a hill just outside of Jerusalem to crucify him. They nailed his hands and feet to a wooden cross then lifted the cross upright into a hole in the ground. Above his head they nailed a sign that said, "Jesus of Nazareth, King of the Jews." Two robbers were crucified with Jesus. By nine o'clock in the morning the soldiers had done their job and sat down to wait for the prisoners to die. While they waited, they threw dice for Jesus' coat. The religious leaders came to jeer at Jesus, "If you are God's Son, let's see you save yourself now!"

Jesus looked down at all this and said, "Father forgive them. They do not know what they are doing."

One of the robbers joined the crowd taunting Jesus, "If you are God's Son, save yourself and save us, too!" But the other robber defended Jesus, "Be quiet! We deserve what we are getting. Jesus does not." Then he turned to Jesus and said, "Remember me when you come as God's King." Jesus looked at him thoughtfully and promised, "You will be with me today in paradise."

At noon, a deep darkness fell across the land and lasted until three o'clock. At that time, Jesus cried out, "It is finished!" Then a few minutes later, "Into you hands I put my spirit." And, his head fell lifeless on his chest.

The captain of the soldiers, who had watched everything, said quietly, "Surely, this man was the Son of God." And many people began to feel afraid.

—*Based on Luke 23:26-49 (NRSV)*

Jesus Is Buried

That evening a rich disciple named Joseph from the town of Arimathea went and asked for Jesus' body. Pilate gave orders for it to he given to Joseph, who took the body and wrapped it in a clean linen cloth. Then Joseph put the body in his own tomb that had been cut into solid rock and had never been used. He rolled a big stone against the entrance of the tomb and went away.

—*Matthew 27:57-60 (CEV)*

chapter seven

Keeping Good Friday

Good Friday is perhaps the last day of the church year on which congregations want to think about the children. It is hard enough to explore the story with adults. We want to protect the children from the sordid details of the day and we fear they will ask questions we have difficulty answering for ourselves much less answering in ways that will make sense to them. But paired with the resurrection story, the crucifixion is the central story of the faith. We have to share it. Just as the Last Supper has more power on Maundy Thursday, the crucifixion has more power on Good Friday. When we deny children the opportunity to explore the crucifixion stories on Good Friday, we do them a great disservice.

This chapter explores three ways congregations can invite children to keep Good Friday. First, congregations can invite children and their families to participate in Good Friday worship that is planned with the presence of children as well as adults in mind. Second, congregations can plan Good Friday events or worship especially for elementary children and their parents. And, third, congregations can encourage families to pay attention to Good Friday at home. Before reading further, you might want to reread the commentary on the crucifixion in chapter 1, pages 13–15.

Including Children in the Congregation's Worship

Because preschoolers are not ready to explore the crucifixion in detail and because they tend to be either overwhelmed by or totally oblivious to the somber mood of the day's worship, they do better to hear the stories in church school and at home. Good childcare is the place for them during Good Friday worship at church. Elementary school children, however, find in the somberness of a Good Friday service proof that the church does indeed take this story very seriously. They are also ready to hear more and more of the details of the texts for the day. Since many of them are out of school on Good Friday, it is possible for them to join in the midday services many congregations hold.

Stripping the sanctuary of all paraments, even large dossal curtains, and draping the central cross with black cloth can be a striking visual statement about the day. If these changes make a noticeable difference in your sanctuary, they lead children to ask "why?" If the changes do not make a striking difference in your sanctuary, they need to be pointed out and explained. While changing the paraments from green to purple during worship is a good option at the beginning of Lent, it is better to strip the sanctuary before the Good Friday service. The one possible exception is to veil the central cross in black immediately after the crucifixion text is read.

To make Good Friday worship more effective for children (and adults too), focus on storytelling rather than preaching. Children especially appreciate hearing the stories of betrayal and desertion that led up to the actual crucifixion. There are several ways to do this.

Tenebrae with its readings and snuffed candles can be celebrated at its original time on Good Friday evening instead of after communion on Maundy Thursday (see directions in chapter 6). When Tenebrae is the main feature of worship, each reading may be followed by a confession. This confession might be a brief prayer of confession related to the story just read. For example, following the reading about Pilate:

> Lord of the cross,
> too often we, like Pilate, wash our hands when we should take action.
> We decide that we can do nothing to change what we know to be wrong.
> We do not try to help people who are being hurt.
> Forgive us.

Or, it might be a repeated verbal or sung confession. The traditional confessional response can be sung in either English, "Lord, have mercy; Christ, have mercy," or Greek, "Kyrie eleison, Christe eleison." One stunning format for this response on Good Friday is for a soloist to sing each phrase with the congregation echoing the soloist as a candle is snuffed following each reading.

Soloist:	Kyrie eleison
Congregation:	**Kyrie eleison**
Soloist:	Christe eleison
Congregation:	**Christe eleison**
Soloist:	Kyrie eleison
Congregation:	**Kyrie eleison**

Though children quickly pick up the response in worship, the experience will be more meaningful for them if the format is introduced and the melody practiced before worship. This can be done in church school classes or during choir rehearsals. It can also be done with the whole congregation before the service begins.

Tenebrae readings are followed by a brief meditation and an affirmation of faith related to the crucifixion. One worship tradition is that no benediction is pronounced on Good Friday because closure of Good Friday worship cannot come until Easter morning. When this is explained and worshipers leave in silence, older children enjoy looking forward to Easter's benediction. The box on page 89 presents one order for such a service.

Special care needs to be taken in selecting Good Friday hymns. Children grasp and sing with fervor the storytelling hymns. "Were You There When They Crucified My Lord?" with its simple language and repeated phrases is the very best Good Friday hymn for children. While the language of "Go to Dark Gethsemane" is more challenging, older children appreciate the story it tells and the call in the last line of each verse to learn from Jesus' story. The African American hymns whose deep emotions are carried more in the music than the words speak powerfully to children. In addition to "Were You There," "He Never Said a Mumbling Word" and "Calvary" bathe children in the feelings of the day. On the other hand, the heavy emotional language of hymns such as "Alas and Did My Savior Bleed and Die" or "In the Cross of Christ I Glory" can confuse and embarrass children. Phrases such as "thus might I hide my blushing face while his dear cross appears" bring to their minds more mushy passions and can lead to rolled eyes and pokes in the ribs. Of these hymns, "Beneath the Cross of Jesus" is perhaps the best choice. Finally, the classical crucifixion hymns tend toward abstract theology and are filled with obsolete vocabulary. For example, "Your mortal sorrow and your life's oblation" and similar phrases make "Ah Holy Jesus" tough for children to understand.

This said, each congregation sings one or two of the not-very-child-friendly Good Friday hymns with an intensity that leads children to conclude that these are very important songs. Even when they do not fully understand their meaning, children try to sing the songs and grow into them. Teachers and choir directors who identify these hymns for their congregation and help children learn them do the children a service. Preachers can help by referring to the hymns in sermons, even structuring a sermon around a particular crucifixion hymn during Lent.

Call to Worship

Hymn

Judas' Betrayal

Congregational Response

Peter's Denials

Congregational Response

Pilate Sentences Jesus

Congregational Response

The Crucifixion

Congregational Response

The Burial

Congregational Response

Meditation

Hymn

Affirmation of Faith

Congregation leaves in silence

A Service or Event Especially for Children and Their Families

Larger congregations and congregations with large numbers of children may want to plan Good Friday services or events especially for elementary children. There are several possibilities.

The Journey Through Holy Week, described in the chapter on Palm/Passion Sunday, could be a Good Friday event. Doing it on a weekday could make it easier to move around the church and make more desirable space available for the children's use. It, however, requires lots of adult or youth leadership that may be harder to secure for a Friday than for a Sunday.

A Tenebrae can be planned and conducted especially for children. Rather than snuff a candle after each reading, present a prop related to each reading as it is read. Readers are seated at a table at the front of the room as in all tenebraes. In front of each reader there is a prop related to that story and a folded black napkin. Readers are seated in story sequence from left to right. As usual, include readers of many different ages. As each reader begins, an older child acolyte picks up the prop for that story, holds it high and solemnly walks a prescribed path among the worshipers so that all can see the prop. If the reader has not finished when the acolyte gets back to the front of the room, the acolyte stands to one side of the table until the reader finishes. If the reader finishes before the acolyte returns, the acolyte slowly continues the full circuit in silence. The acolyte then returns the prop to its place on the table and covers it with the black napkin. If the napkin is arranged so a corner hangs over the front of the table, a pattern of black grows across the table as the readings continue. A deep toned bell (perhaps a handbell) is tolled once as the acolyte steps back into place following each reading. A rehearsal is essential.

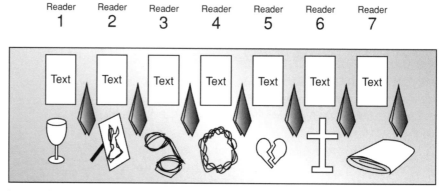

Set up Schematic

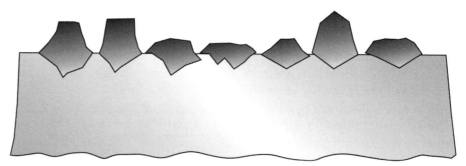

Front View: End of Service

Props can be determined by what is available in church closets. The following list is used in one congregation with an annual children's Tenebrae:

- **The Last Supper:** a communion chalice
- **Jesus Prays in the Garden:** picture of Jesus praying in the garden displayed on table easel
- **Jesus Is Arrested:** a length of rope with ends tied in loops (The acolyte slips the loops over her wrists leaving them hooked over her thumbs so they will not slip all the way down her arms.)
- **Jesus Is Sentenced to Death:** crown of thorns made from whatever thorny vines grow in your area
- **Peter's Denials:** a large red cardboard broken heart (The acolyte carries one half of the broken heart in each hand holding the halves close to each other to show the heart shape.)
- **Jesus Is Killed:** a freestanding cross
- **Jesus Is Buried:** a length of white fabric carried draped across the acolyte's arms

This child's tenebrae is the heart of a very simple order of worship that lasts about a half hour (see box). The call to worship is a greeting by the worship leader, noting the importance of the day and pointing out what will happen. A children's choir may add an anthem. Adults will be needed to accompany the hymns, but an older child or teenager playing an instrument such as flute or violin may enrich their accompaniment.

It is also possible to provide a Good Friday gathering for children and their families that is not a worship service. Such events usually include some storytelling, some singing and a cross craft. The feel of the event is a merger of worship and a church school class.

As worshipers arrive they are invited to work on a craft project related to the cross. The possibilities are almost endless and include the following:

Greeting
Hymn: "Open My Eyes That I May See"
Readings
Hymn: "Were You There?"
Prayer
Send worshipers out in silence, waiting for Easter

God's Eyes: Yarn is wrapped around the arms of a cross to form a diamond-shaped eye. The cross is made of two plastic straws lashed together with heavy thread or craft sticks glued together. Spray paint the crosses gold before the children arrive. Tie the yarn to the cross at the cross point and start it by wrapping the yarn around each cross arm in sequence for several rounds to form the center of the eye. Children continue what you have begun. To emphasize the mood of Good Friday select yarn in somber colors, maybe black and silver or deep purple. Or, to emphasize the "good" in Good Friday, follow the Central American God's eye tradition by selecting brightly colored yarns.

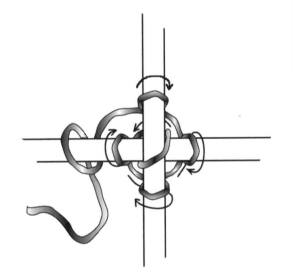

Hot Crossed Buns: If a snack is to be shared at the end of the session, paint white icing crosses on sweet rolls with new paintbrushes. Children may prepare just enough for participants at the event or each child may prepare a small plate of rolls to take home to their families.

Wooden crosses to carry all weekend: Give each child a precut wood cross (approximately four inches by two and a half inches) and a piece of fine sandpaper with which to sand it smooth. Also provide small rags to soak in linseed oil and rub into the wood.

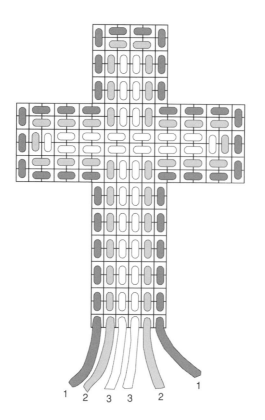

Weave colored yarn or narrow ribbon into crosses cut from nylon mesh: Precut crosses approximately four inches by eight inches. Give children black or purple ribbons (#2 and #3 in the illustration) to weave into it today and a length of gold or white with metallic gold in it (#1 in the illustration) to add around the edge on Easter Sunday. The number of holes in each arm of the cross is more important to three-ribbon success than the measurements of the netting. Each arm and the top should be six holes long and wide. The base should be six holes wide and twelve holes tall. Tell the children to leave the outside border of holes empty for the Easter ribbon.

When all have arrived and had time to work on crosses, gather the group for storytelling and singing.

With a group of fewer than thirty, one of the best ways to work through the Passion stories is to present the children with plastic Easter eggs filled with reminders of the stories. This may be commercially produced "Resurrection Eggs" or a homemade set of eggs. Open the eggs together in story sequence. Ask children to tell the story each prop recalls. Work as a group to recall all the details of the story and to correct misunderstandings. Have a Good News Translation or Contemporary English Version of the Bible available, with each story marked ready for quick reference as needed. This informal setting allows the leader to open conversations about the stories. "I wonder what Peter was thinking as he ran away crying?" "I wonder how Pilate felt after he washed his hands and sent Jesus to die?" The leader's "I wonder" questions challenge children to think about the stories and give them the opportunity to raise their own "I wonder" questions.

In larger groups, it is easier to read a story than to deal with small props the children in the back cannot see. The story may be carefully selected Bible texts or a Bible storybook. The storybook may be focused on the passion or may trace the entire life of Jesus including the crucifixion and resurrection.

Palm Leaf Cross: It is possible to combine the cross craft and the Bible story by making crosses out of palm leaves. There are directions for making this cross with a series of precise folds, but they are both difficult to understand and hard to carry out. The easier approach is simply to tie a knot at the appropriate place in two palm fronds and then trim the leaves if needed. Give the children each two palm leaves while recalling the Palm Sunday story. Let them hold the leaves as you tell of the crowd's cry "Crucify him!" and the jeering at the cross. Show the children how to tie the leaves to form a cross and encourage them to display their palm cross in their bedroom as it dries out. If Ash Wednesday is celebrated in your congregation, describe the practice of making the ashes by burning the previous year's palms. (This might also serve as a children's message in a congregation-wide Good Friday service.)

While the focus is on the crucifixion, it is possible to add a second, related story. There are a small number of *midrashim*, or stories about the story, to help children understand the meaning of the cross. *The Tale of Three Trees*, by Angelia Elwell Hunt, describes the dreams of three trees growing on a hilltop. The dream of each tree is realized in a surprising way in the life of Jesus. The third, of course, becomes the cross. A carefully prepared leader can read *The Giving Tree*, by Shel Silverstein, and compare that tree to Jesus' "giving tree," the cross. The story in Bob Hartmann's *The Easter Angels* focuses on the two angels who were sent to the tomb on Easter morning, but it could be read on Good Friday to explore the significance of Jesus' death on the cross. Help children identify how the angels felt about death in general and Jesus' death in particular as they sat waiting for the women in the garden. Then discuss how they felt when they learned of God's Easter surprise. Finally, invite the children to ponder what the angels learned about death from Jesus' death and resurrection.

Follow the story and discussions by a brief prayer and perhaps sing "Were You There?"

Prepare Families to Note Good Friday on Their Own

Many family schedules make getting to Good Friday worship at the church difficult. Some will be on traveling on long holiday weekends from school. If such families are to keep Good Friday and Easter, they must be both encouraged and resourced by their congregations.

In newsletter articles and letters to parents, congregations can point out the need for children to hear the passion stories that come between Palm Sunday and Easter. Brief descriptions of how children understand the cross help parents who are unsure about sharing this story with children and provide ideas about what they might say. Some years, parent workshops, or classes like those described in Part 3, offer parents extensive help. Other years, an especially good children's account of Holy Week can be mailed to each family. Still other years, a simple letter with suggestions for celebrating Holy Week at home or on the road may be sent. All of these efforts let parents know that keeping Good Friday and Easter with their children is important.

Keeping Good Friday as a family does not need to be a major undertaking. The primary activity is simply reading or telling the story sometime during the day. This may be done at a meal, at bedtime, or during a usual quiet, story time. This reading and a brief conversation about the significance of the day are all that is needed. There was a time when Christians severely curtailed their activities on Good Friday. Seamstresses said, "A hem stitched on Good Friday will never hang right." Many fasted. While few families want to go to such extremes, many can plan to eat simple meals, avoid parties, and watch only videos selected to fit the day. It is also a good day to eat hot-crossed buns. Simply paint icing crosses on store-bought or home-made sweet rolls.

When children worship with their families at church on Good Friday or read and discuss the crucifixion with their families at home, they are ready to participate more fully in the celebration of the resurrection on Easter morning.

A Newsletter Article

How Do I Explain Easter to My Children (or Grandchildren)?

A good starting point is to realize that Easter is bigger than any of us ever fully understand so we do not have to know all the answers. No one ever does. Easter is new life, an empty tomb, forgiveness, resurrection, and more. That is not something to understand. It is a reality we have to grow into. The truth is that we understand different aspects of Easter better at different times of our lives.

Adults respond enthusiastically to the Easter claim and promise of victory over death because adults understand the finality of death and fear death. Children, however, have a hard time grasping the reality, especially the finality, of death. Even after attending Grandpa's funeral, a young child will often ask, at unexpected times, when Grandpa will be visiting. This natural inability to grasp the finality of death is supported by fairy tale princesses who awake after "sleeping" for years and cartoon characters who, flattened by steamrollers, peel themselves off the road. Given all this, it's not surprising that children can't get too excited by victory over death.

Many books and people try to get around this by focusing on new life, paying attention to eggs, bulbs, and butterflies as new life symbols. While children are vaguely interested in these symbols, "new life" strikes few of them (for whom all of life is "new") as particularly significant or exciting.

Instead, for younger children, the empty tomb is the ultimate victory of the good guys (God/Jesus) over the bad guys (Judas, the priests, Pilate, the soldiers). On Good Friday the bad guys thought they had won. They killed Jesus and sealed his body into a guarded tomb. On Easter morning God/Jesus blasted right out of that tomb and proved once and for all that God is more powerful than even the worst evil the worst bad guys can inflict. The natural response to such a victory is to yell "Hooray for God and Jesus!" and to celebrate belonging to God who is the most powerful power there is in the universe!

To older elementary children, who are focused on friendships and have clear expectations of "best friends," the most significant resurrection story is the story of Peter's breakfast conversation with Jesus (see John 21:1-19). Peter had been Jesus' best friend. He had promised to stick with Jesus no matter what. And he had been caught three times on the same night pretending he did not even know Jesus. As a betrayed "best friend," Jesus would have been justified in ignoring or punishing Peter for his denials. But Jesus did not. For Peter, the resurrection happened when Jesus forgave him, welcomed him back as a friend, and put him to work building God's Kingdom. For older children, Easter holds the promise that Jesus will forgive them and welcome them back when/if they betray their friendship with him. Such Easter forgiveness is worth celebrating!

And remember the starting point—Easter is bigger than we can understand. We don't have to know all the answers. We probably do most harm when we fail to talk with our children about our Easter faith out of fear that we will not get it right. This Easter season our congregation especially invites children and their families to . . .

chapter eight

The Church-Sponsored Easter Egg Hunt

It is time for the churches to take back the Easter egg hunts. Civic groups, clubs, and even county recreation departments in most communities have taken them over with the best of intentions. Unfortunately, because the sponsors are civic rather than religious, they have focused on prizes for most eggs, finding prize eggs, and photo ops or breakfast with costumed Easter bunnies. While these events can be fun and draw large crowds, they are really only egg hunts, not Easter egg hunts. Attendees leave with no idea why they have gone hunting for eggs.

As Christians we hunt Easter eggs not because the Easter Bunny brings them to us, but because they remind us of God's Easter surprise. Actually the colored plastic eggs that most children receive at Easter today present this reminder more clearly to young children than dyed hardboiled eggs did. On the third day the women went to the tomb worrying about how they would open that tomb to get to the dead body of Jesus; instead they found the tomb already opened and Jesus resurrected. That was a surprise! Usually eggs are white and when you crack them open you find an egg yoke. But at Easter eggs come in every color and when you crack them open you find candies and prizes. That is also a surprise!

An Easter egg hunt that includes telling the empty tomb story in a way that explains why we hunt eggs at Easter can be an important way to celebrate the empty tomb with young children and their families. It may actually be the only opportunity the church will have to tell this story to some preschoolers. It is also a chance to tell the story to parents in a way that they can retell to their children later.

The following story, "God's Easter Surprise," has evolved from several years of Easter egg stories. It can be retold each year to an appreciative audience.

The story plus the egg hunt are all that is necessary for a very successful and significant event. This is definitely a case in which less is better. Adding a whole spring festival of face painting, pony rides, and games only dilutes the meaning of the eggs. Costumed bunnies or any mention of the Easter Bunny are to be avoided not because the church is anti-bunny, but because the church is pro-Jesus. The bunny gets plenty of attention elsewhere.

God's Easter Surprise

Jesus was just full of surprises.

When he saw mean little Zaccheus sitting up in a tree, he stopped and called up to him, "Surprise, Zaccheus! God loves you. I want to be your friend."

When it was lunchtime for a whole crowd and only one boy had a lunch box, Jesus said, "Surprise! There is always enough to go around when we share." Then, he split that lunch so everyone had enough to eat.

When Jesus saw a blind man, he said, "Surprise!" and healed his eyes.

Jesus also said some surprising things.

He said, "God loves everyone – even the people you do not like."

He said, "God wants us to share."

He said, "Love people who are mean to you."

Finally, some people had enough of Jesus and all his surprises. They said, "We'd feel better if Jesus were not around." So they killed him. They put his dead body in a cave AND rolled a big rock across the door AND put an official "Stay Out" sticker on the rock AND put two soldiers on guard duty. "That will take care of Jesus and his surprises," they said.

Jesus' friends were very, very sad. They cried on Friday when Jesus was killed. They cried on Saturday and hid out at home. They were still crying on Sunday morning when they went to the cave tomb. But when they got there:

SURPRISE! No soldiers.

SURPRISE! The big rock was rolled away from the door.

SURPRISE! Jesus' dead body was gone.

SURPRISE! Two angels were there and they said,

"SURPRISE! Jesus is not here! He is not dead any more! He has risen!"

Surprise, surprise, surprise! Jesus was right. God's love is bigger and stronger than we can ever guess.

The Easter word for all those surprises is "Alleluia!" And that makes me think of a song we all know, "Praise Ye the Lord, Alleluia!" *(If your children do not know this song or another song with lots of alleluias in it, skip this and move on to the next paragraph.)*

One more Easter surprise: What is usually inside an egg? *(Crack an egg into a glass dish held by a child. Hear children's response to the yolk.)*

NOT ON EASTER! On Easter you can hardly guess what is in an egg: candy, stickers, erasers…*(Crack a plastic egg open and spill its contents into another child's hands.)* I understand that there are hundreds of surprise eggs. *(Give directions for the hunt itself.)*

If we do not focus on Jesus at church, the children will never know he is involved in Easter at all. The one possible happy addition to a Saturday morning egg hunt is a family breakfast—probably pancakes. The whole event—breakfast ending with the story told while families are still at their tables, directly followed by the egg hunt—takes a little over an hour and provides great fellowship for families.

Egg Hunt Logistics

Everyone has more fun on an egg hunt when there are clear age divisions. A small grassy area with clear boundaries is all that is needed for children younger than three. Three-year-olds through seven-year-olds enjoy large spaces in which they can scoop up a number of eggs quickly and some trees, rocks, and other objects that provide true hiding places for eggs. It is important to have an upper age limit. One way to enforce this limit is to give jobs to older brothers and sisters who are along but too old to hunt. They can help hide eggs or assist the storyteller by holding the egg dish.

Egg hunts require lots of plastic eggs. *Instruct parents and children to empty their surprises into their Easter baskets and then put their eggshells into big boxes near the hunt area.* Also watch for the after-Easter sales to pick up additional eggs at a good price.

What do you put in the eggshells? A grand variety of small treasures and candies. The joy of the occasion is best served if all eggs are different but fairly equal. Prize eggs only cause preschoolers unnecessary grief. There are a few, obvious, once-you-think-about-it cautions:

- All candies must be individually wrapped for sanitation.
- Chocolate candies melt very quickly while lying in the sun.
- No toys or candies of a size that might present a choking hazard to children younger than three.

Be thoughtful in selecting religious toys and candies. There are some amazing things on the market for Christian children at Easter. Not all of them are theologically thoughtful. Take a moment to ask yourself, what does my child think while slurping a cross shaped lollipop, eating chocolate praying hands, or playing with a cheap "Jesus Is Risen" yo-yo that will quickly break? Most of us will react differently to different items. General guidelines are that any printed messages should make sense to children and that there should be some sense of reverence involved in the use of Christian symbols. Finally, read the verbal messages that come with the currently popular color-coded jellybeans. Not all messages are the same. You may want to create a color-coding that fits your understanding of the Easter message for children.

Packing all these goodies into hundreds of eggshells is a job for a group, not one volunteer going solo. Youth (even older elementary) groups or church school classes, women's circles, or parents waiting for children in choir rehearsals can stuff eggs while they visit, or pursue lessons or business together. They do need detailed instructions about how many items to put in each egg. If stickers are one of the surprises, tell the stuffers to put the stickers in the eggs for the children to use rather than use them to decorate or seal the eggs on the outside.

It does occasionally rain or snow on an Easter egg hunt. Rather than reschedule, move indoors. The younger than three-year-olds can happily hunt their eggs in any open space—a large room or wide hallway do fine. The older children delight in searching for eggs that can be more creatively hidden in all the nooks and crannies provided by a couple of children's classrooms. Just be sure to state clearly that all eggs are in full view so there is no need to open doors or move things. Also be sure to have a "straighten things up committee" to leave rooms ready for Easter Sunday morning.

chapter nine

Easter Sunday

Easter Sunday is a challenging day for people responsible for the church's children. Sheer numbers are often a problem. Providing adequate space and adult leadership to meet the needs of unusually large crowds of children can be daunting. Since a significant number of the children in the crowd (1) are not "regulars" and therefore do not know how things go here, (2) are dressed in new and often uncomfortable clothes, and (3) have feasted on sweets all morning, the challenge grows. Finally, the story of the day is both unfamiliar and unusual to say the least. Sharing God's Easter message with this crowd of children requires careful planning.

This chapter is closely related to and builds on chapters 1 and 2. If you have not already read them, stop now to read the commentaries in chapter 1 on the empty tomb and resurrection stories (pages 15–22) and the descriptions of how children of each age respond to and celebrate the Easter stories in chapter 2. They are the background around which these pragmatic suggestions for Easter Sunday morning are designed.

The Infant and Toddler Nurseries

Many parents who have given birth to a late fall or winter baby and parents who have stayed out of the church nursery to avoid winter bugs that children share there bring their child to the church nursery on Easter with both hopes and fears. If the day goes well for them and their child, they are likely to return. If the day does not go well, they often decide to wait until their child is older before any of them return to church. That makes it an important day to have the church nurseries in tiptop form. More than Easter Sunday is at stake.

The rooms need to be exceptionally clean and well equipped. They also need to be decorated for Easter: an Easter lily prominently displayed, Easter music playing quietly in the background, plastic eggshells for older infants and toddlers to play with, and a picture of Jesus announce to everyone who enters the room that Easter is being celebrated here. These children are not just being efficiently warehoused while their adults celebrate Easter. They are part of the congregation's celebration of Easter.

Adult leaders (often parent volunteers) also need to be prepared. Without direction, most volunteers will treat their work as simple childcare, a necessary task if most parents are to be free to worship in the sanctuary. With direction they can be challenged to celebrate Easter with the children. A letter to Easter volunteers thanking them and offering some very specific suggestions is often all it takes. See the sample below. To give volunteers a fuller vision, print the paragraphs from pages 23–24 on the back of the page. The following copyright notice and credit line must appear on each copy: "From *Sharing the Easter Faith with Children* by Carolyn C. Brown. © 2005 Abingdon Press. Reproduced by permission."

Easter in the Nursery at *(Name of Church)*

Thank you for serving as a nursery volunteer on Easter Sunday.

You are scheduled to serve on _Date_ in _Room_ at _Time_. Remember that people will arrive early to get seats so please be in your room by _Time_ for the _Service_. (Include time for finding a parking place.) If for any reason, you cannot be here, please call _Name_ at _Number_ as soon as possible.

This is not just any Sunday. It is Easter Sunday. Even the infants and toddlers sense the difference. The nursery will be freshly cleaned and well stocked with supplies. It will also be decorated. We encourage you to celebrate Easter with these youngest members of the congregation in the following ways:

- Greet each parent and child with "Happy Easter!" Introduce yourself and be sure you know both parents' and children's names as they sign in.
- There will be an Easter lily and a picture of Jesus prominently displayed in the nursery. Show them to the children one on one throughout the morning. Talk about Jesus and the pretty Easter flower to children as you walk them or rock them. Though they will not remember what you say, they will begin having happy associations with church and Jesus. A good start!
- There will be Easter music CDs playing quietly in the background. Keep them going. Sing along occasionally with songs you know.
- Play with the Easter word "Alleluia!" Show a baby how to say the word with exaggerated lip and tongue motions. Even infants will watch you closely and move their tongues a little in response. It is a fun Easter activity for the changing table and a good way to distract a child who is getting weepy. Try this. It is fun.

On the back of this page are a few paragraphs explaining why we go to the extra effort on behalf of our youngest children.

Again, thank you for serving in the nursery on Easter Sunday. We hope it will be a good day for you as well as for the children.

—The Nursery Committee

Sharing Easter with Preschoolers

For young children Easter is one part story and one part happy response. The youngest children simply join in on the happy activities and feelings of the day. Because the sanctuary is the place where Easter joy has its fullest expression, it is important for young children to visit the sanctuary on Easter. Families and church school classes can go see the massed lilies and look at Easter banners. They can tiptoe in to listen to trumpeters or choirs practicing. Worship service nursery groups can even listen to the congregation singing Easter hymns from a side door propped open for a few minutes. All these short visits include children in Easter joy now and pave the way for their presence in the sanctuary in a few years.

As they grow, children get as interested in the story as in the joy. They hear and explore that story best in classrooms with other children. Most church school curriculums provide ample resources for the exploration during the church school hour. On Easter Sunday, though, the majority of preschoolers will appear not during church school, but during worship. It is therefore important to present the Easter story during the worship nurseries. Children who hear it twice, once in church school and again during a worship hour, are twice as likely to grasp it. If the congregation does not usually provide planned learning activities during worship hours, this is a day to make an exception.

In the hour plus available, plan a joint story time followed by an in-class craft activity and an Easter snack. Begin by gathering three-, four-, and five-year-olds to share in an Easter story time. (Let the leader of the two-year-olds decide if they can handle moving to another room and being with a larger crowd of children without major meltdowns.) One well-prepared storyteller equipped with scenery and props can tell the story with dramatic effect. This time together need not be more than ten minutes. See the sample story on pages 102–3.

Back in classrooms children share a special snack, probably an Easter sugar cookie, then work on a craft. The craft suggested here is making Easter cards. Before Sunday, egg-shaped Easter card shells are prepared. Fold pastel colored construction paper in half and cut into a large egg shape with the fold running down one side. Print "Jesus is Alive! Happy Easter!" inside each egg.

Children decorate outside

On Sunday, the children decorate the front and back of the eggs using markers, crayons, glitter pens, stickers, bits of lace and ribbon—whatever the supply closet and your imagination can supply. They will take the cards to parents or friends. If there is extra time, classroom volunteers can read provided Easter storybooks.

When the plans for the morning are communicated to them in writing the week before and all their supplies are provided in their classrooms, volunteers who usually "just baby-sit" are happy to provide the needed leadership and enjoy hearing the Easter story told well in an age-appropriate way.

Easter Story Time

Setting

Use a large enough room for children to sit on the floor, close together but not crowded. An upright piano and bench is set up as the closed tomb (see Directions below) with a few Easter lilies around it. A recording of outdoor sounds plays in the background as children arrive.

Singing

Sing one or two songs of praise that are familiar to the children.

The Story

Today we have a story from the Bible. It starts out very sad and ends up very, very happy. It starts on a Friday. There were some people who did not like Jesus. They were really angry with him—so angry that they decided to kill him on a cross. This is what it looked like. *(Present a picture of the crucifixion, taking care that all can see it well)* It was a very sad day. Jesus' friends cried and cried. God was sad too. But God also had a big surprise waiting. Jesus' friends took his body off the cross, wrapped it gently in a big white sheet, and *(Turn toward tomb set)* laid it in a cave tomb. A big rock was rolled across the door so no one could get in.

On Sunday morning three women went to the tomb. They wanted to leave good-smelling spices near Jesus' body. Were they surprised when they got there! The stone was rolled back! *(Push the stone aside)* The tomb was open! *(Look inside)* Jesus' body was gone! All that was there was the big sheet they had wrapped around his body—AND—an angel. *(Turn as if facing the angel)*

The angel said, "Why are you looking for Jesus in a tomb for dead people? He is not here! He is risen!"

The women ran to find Jesus' friends Peter and John. *(Run to a corner of the room)* Peter and John ran to the tomb and looked in. *(Run back to the tomb and look in)* They were confused. *(Scratch head in confusion)* They just did not understand. They went back home trying to figure out what happened.

Mary sat down on the stone *(Sit on the stone)* and cried. She cried and cried and cried. She did not even look up when someone asked her, "Woman, why are you crying?"

(Cry into your hands) "...because Jesus is dead, and, and I just don't understand, and..."

"Mary." *(Look up)* Mary knew that voice. It couldn't be, but it was . . . "Jesus?"

"Yes," Jesus said. "It is me. I am alive. I have risen. Now go tell Peter and John and all the others."

And Mary did run and tell everyone she met. *(Run from child to child)* "(Name), Jesus is alive!" and "(Name), Jesus has risen! I saw him!" *(Try to address the children by name)*

As she went Mary began singing, (start singing) "Allelu, Allelu, Praise Ye the Lord." At first she sang it loudly. *(Whole group sings it loudly)* Then all Jesus' friends sang it together happily. *(Whole group sings it happily)* That night as she went to bed, she sang it softly as she fell asleep. *(Whole group sings it softly)*.

Let's pray an Easter prayer. *(Fold your hands)* Thank you, God, for Easter day. We are so happy that Jesus is alive now and always. Alleluia! Amen.

Directions for Cave Tomb Set: *An upright piano and bench can be made into a cave tomb. Turn the piano so that the keyboard faces the area where the children will sit. The area under the keyboard serves as the cave. Swathe the whole piano in gray-brown bulletin board paper or rough cloth (gray or brown burlap). Be sure that the lower side of the keyboard and "sides of the cave" are completely covered. Lay a white sheet on the floor of the cave. Also cover the bench. It becomes the stone rolled across the door. Place a few Easter lilies and other live or artificial plants around the tomb to complete the garden effect.*

Elementary Children

Elementary school children are ready to join the congregation for Easter worship and to explore the stories with increasing detail. In worship they sense the Easter joy and begin claiming Easter traditions and hymns of their congregation. Worship is, however, not the best place for them to explore the biblical stories. Because Easter preaching tends to jump immediately from the story to pondering its meaning in fairly abstract terms, it often goes over the heads of the children. The children do better exploring the stories at their own pace in classrooms and then "hearing it again" in the sanctuary. That makes both worship and church school important Easter activities for elementary children.

Possibly the best worship experience for these story-oriented children is *a sunrise service set in a cemetery, memorial garden, or by the church's columbarium.* A smaller shorter service, set on the congregation's property and focused on story-telling and liturgy more than preaching, has greater impact on children than most larger community services. A half-hour sunrise service, followed by an informal breakfast of Easter pastries, is a great way for a family to start Easter day.

The time and location set the stage for the story. There are numerous dramatic reading scripts and skits available. But the story is so stark, and the emotions involved so hard to portray, that dramatic presentations often come off as hokey. Reading the account from a good Bible storybook is often a better choice. In one effective sunrise telling of the story, the congregation sang the first verse of "Were You There?" followed by the reading of "Mary of Magdala Sees Jesus" (*The Family Story Bible*, by Ralph Milton). The story works well with the song, beginning with Mary at the cross. Then the congregation sang "Jesus Christ Is Risen Today," providing a way for worshipers to join Mary in her joy. This particular presentation of the Word was set within the usual liturgical order for that congregation, with care taken that the language of the prayers and other hymns be child friendly.

When singing out of doors, it can be difficult to create a robust Easter sound. Few musicians want to roll a piano out into the morning damp and if they do, the sound tends to be "small." So this is a great opportunity to include older children and youth playing trumpets, horns, even drums to back up a keyboard player. An intergenerational handbell choir, assembled specifically for that service, graced one sunrise service I attended.

When Easter sunrise or early morning services for families must be inside, children respond well to changing the paraments as a featured part of worship. This service begins with the sanctuary stripped for Good Friday. Sing a verse or two of "Were You There?" and hear the story of Jesus' burial. Then announce that the story does not end there. Change the paraments on the lectern under the Bible and the worship garb of the reader, with ceremony and comments, before reading the empty tomb story. Follow the reading with an Easter hymn, during which other paraments and worship garb are changed. If the "alleluia" was buried at the beginning of Lent, bring it out and follow with a litany featuring lots of congregational "alleluias." Lilies can be added with the paraments or during a sermon exploring the surprise Easter lilies contain. Or families can be invited to place the lilies at the conclusion of the service. This worship plan draws the attention of the children to both the story and the ways we respond to it in Easter worship. It educates the children and helps them share the Easter joy.

Many children and their families will, however, worship in the sanctuary later on Easter morning. Sparkly white and gold paraments and banners, Easter lilies, and special music draw the interest of these children. Explaining their significance during worship builds children's appreciation and sense of inclusion in the celebration. If an "alleluia" was buried at the beginning of Lent, be sure to bring it out with a flourish, perhaps before singing a hymn filled with alleluias. Challenging children to count all the alleluias in the service and tell the minister at the door also invites children to pay attention. If the minister offers each child who counts the alleluias an Easter candy from his or her pocket, children know they are wanted in the sanctuary!

Trumpets add special triumph to the day. Trumpeters may play special anthems and accompany the congregation on Easter hymns. They may also play a part in unique calls to worship. For example, a trumpet fanfare may be answered by a series of congregational responses preceding the first hymn.

In all these "out of the ordinary" liturgical events, children feel the congregation's Easter joy and share in it.

Trumpet fanfare

Worship Leader: Christ is risen!

Trumpet fanfare

Congregation: Christ is risen, indeed!

Trumpet fanfare

All: Let us worship God.

While thoughtfully planned Easter liturgy invites children to participate, few Easter sermons make much sense to them. To explore the biblical stories at their own level, they depend on *church school classes* and family discussions. Most church school curriculums offer excellent resources for doing this. The challenge for the congregation is to be sure these resources get used. Too often church school classes are shortened or even cancelled to make way for large worship crowds or to prepare children's choirs to sing in worship. Teachers, faced with shorter than usual times or unsure of how they will effectively present the story, frequently opt for games and crafts that may avoid the biblical story entirely. Congregations serve the children when they protect the Easter church school hour or intentionally plan for the Easter stories to be explored the following Sunday. They also serve both the teachers and the children when they hold meetings to help teachers understand how they can present the story to their children. (See part 3 for session plans.) Church school may be the only opportunity many children have to hear and explore this story.

The focus of Easter morning is on worship in the sanctuary. Worship committees, pastors, choirs, even custodians pull out all of the stops to make it a spectacular morning. The trick to including children in the congregation's Easter celebration is for the people planning worship in the sanctuary to remember that children will be part of the congregation—AND—for all the adults planning for children who will not be in the sanctuary to put as much enthusiasm into their planning as the worship leaders do into the sanctuary activities. A few leaders who insist that Easter celebration should overflow the sanctuary into classrooms and nurseries can give adult volunteers there a sense of the importance and joy of their work with the children.

PART THREE

Study Sessions for Parents, Teachers, and Worship Committees

Parents and children's church school teachers quickly admit to needing help communicating the Easter message to children effectively. The information in chapters 1 and 2 is provided for them. The following session plans are provided to help them read and explore the material in groups. Sessions A through G can be used individually or in a variety of series. For example: a five-week Lenten church school course for parents could include sessions A, F, C, D, and E. (F is early in the sequence because it deals with Lenten disciplines that are started at the beginning of Lent.) Church school teachers might do session A and/or B during spring teachers' meetings. A worship committee whose members read chapters 1 and 2 in advance might do session G to evaluate their inclusion of children in the congregation's Lent–Easter observances. Other groups will select different sessions or parts of sessions to meet different needs. The hope is that you will be able to tailor programs that meet your unique needs.

Session A: How Children Grow into Lent and Easter

Provide a collection of Lent–Easter objects: a box of pretzel twists, a cross, a large nail, a crown of thorns, a plastic Easter egg, a child's Easter bonnet, an Easter basket, a coin offering box, one purple and one white parament, a palm branch, a chalice, a shallow dish of ashes, an Easter lily, a butterfly banner or picture, a book of Lenten family devotions, and a portrait of Jesus. Invite class members to select one to introduce to the class, explaining briefly what it means or has meant to them as part of Lent–Easter. (Keep this activity to five or so minutes. It is only a way to get people thinking.)

Present chapter 2 as a lecture. The chart at the end of the chapter can be given to students as an outline and a place to write notes. Also, refer to the Lent–Easter items on the table as you work through the ages. For example, "As first graders come to the sanctuary during Lent, they are ready for the dish of ashes, the paraments, the chalice, and . . . *(any other items related to Lenten worship in your congregation)*." This presentation will require the majority of class time.

If your students are mainly parents, give each student a copy of your congregation's calendar for Lent and Easter and any materials that will be available for families to use at home. Ask for a show of hands indicating which events are attended and which resources are used. Discuss ways children are invited to participate in your congregation's celebration of Easter using the following questions:
- Which of these activities and services will be meaningful for which age children?
- How can you take advantage of these activities and use the resources?
- What can your family do at home to enrich your celebration of Lent and Easter?
- What can the church offer that would further enrich your family's celebration of Lent and Easter?

If your students are mainly church school teachers, ask them in advance to bring Lent–Easter curriculum resources with them. Take time for teachers or teaching teams to review upcoming lessons in light of what they have just heard.
- In what ways do the goals for Lenten lessons fit what we have just explored?
- In what ways might we adapt the materials to fit our particular students this year?

Closing: Ask students to look again at the collection of items with which you began and to select from them or add to them two or three items they want to "put on a table" for their children this year during Lent and Easter. Share lists and discuss reasons. Close with prayer for sharing the Easter messages with our children.

Session B: Hearing the Stories from a Child's Point of View

Open with one of the following reviews of the biblical Holy Week stories:

- Display a basket of Resurrection Eggs. Pass out the eggs. Ask students to open the eggs one at the time. (You may want to call for them in the color order listed in the egg carton.) As a group, identify the token in each egg and the story it represents. Have biblical references ready for someone to read should the class be stumped. As you work through the story eggs, compile a list of questions children ask about the stories on a chalkboard or newsprint.

- If your church has a collection of large teaching pictures related to the stories of Holy Week, display them across the front of the room in haphazard order. Invite students to put them in the correct chronological order. The rule is that a student may move only one picture at the time, briefly telling the story behind the picture and noting the reason for the new placement. Be ready to read the biblical text behind any picture that students do not recognize or about which they raise questions. You might keep a list of questions children ask about the stories as you get them into order.

- If your students are quite familiar with the Holy Week stories, invite them to brainstorm a list of Holy Week stories. Record their list on newsprint or a chalkboard. Then put the stories into chronological order by numbering the listed items.

When the review is complete, ask students which of these stories are the hardest to share with children. If you have started a list of questions children ask, add to it. If you have not started the list, do so now. (Whichever activity you select should take no more than ten minutes.)

Assign each "hard story" to a small group. Give them the biblical reference for the story, a commentary, and the excerpt related to it from chapter one. Ask each group to study their story and report to the class their ideas about how to share that story with children. Urge them to report ways their work gives them answers to any of the listed questions children ask.

After all groups have reported, work together to answer any remaining listed questions.

Display, on preprinted newsprint or on a chalkboard, the three basic Easter messages for children.

> Surprise, God's love is the strongest power in the universe!
> God is with us always—even after we die.
> God forgives us!

As a class connect each picture or story from the opening exercise to one of these themes. Challenge students to restate the message of each story in terms of the connected themes.

Closing: In prayer, give thanks for the stories and ask for wisdom in sharing them with the children.

Session C: God's Easter Surprise

Present the class with three Easter symbols: a plastic Easter egg, a butterfly picture or banner, and an Easter lily. Challenge the class to explain the meaning of each symbol and what the symbols have in common. Lead the conversation toward connecting each to the theme of surprise. Surprise—an egg contains candy! Surprise—a cocoon holds a butterfly! Surprise—a bulb holds a flower! (Take five minutes or less for this activity.)

Read aloud the stories of Jesus' death and burial in Matthew 27:26-50 and 57-66. Then briefly discuss how very thoroughly it appeared that Jesus had been defeated on Friday. Ask students to:

* List the humiliations piled on Jesus as he died.
* Imagine what the religious leaders thought as they went home Friday evening.
* Imagine what Jesus' followers thought as they went home Friday evening.

Next, assign small groups of students to read silently one of the following Easter texts:

> Mark 16:1-8 (the empty tomb)
> Luke 24:13-35 (the road to Emmaus)
> Luke 24:36-49 (Jesus appears to disciples)
> John 20:24-29 (Jesus appears to Thomas to prove the surprise)

When all have finished reading, work through the texts as a class, calling on each reading group to identify the surprises in its story and how people responded to the surprise.

Finally, ask students to put God's Easter surprise message into words children can understand by completing the phrase, "Surprise—..." Ask for several examples. Explore the need to understand the apparent completeness of the Good Friday defeat in order to appreciate the joy of the Easter surprise. As a group, name the challenges of sharing both messages with our children and explore ways to meet the challenges.

Read "God's Easter Surprise," the story for the Easter Egg Hunt (page 96), and discuss its teaching use at an egg hunt.

Closing: Read Romans 8:38-39 to the class. Invite students to add to the list of things that cannot separate us from the love of God. In prayer, thank God for the Easter surprise and ask for help in sharing it with the children.

Session D: God Is with Us Always

Read all or parts of the book *Lifetimes: A Beautiful Way to Explain Death to Children*, by Bryan Mellonie and Robert Ingpen (available in most public or school libraries). Point out that while it is a fine introduction to death for children, it is limited for Christians. Present again the egg, butterfly, and lily symbols from the last session. Note that while they say "surprise" most clearly to children, they also say there is new life in surprising places—like eggs, cocoons, bulbs, and an empty tomb.

To explore the story of the Easter experiences of Mary Magdalene, do some or all of the following:

- Read "Mary of Magdala Sees Jesus" in *The Family Story Bible*, by Ralph Milton, or tell the story of Mary from the preschool story time on pages 102–3. Then, give students time to read excerpts from the commentary in chapter one on the empty tomb (pages 15–16) and Mary Magdalene (pages 17–18).
- Read aloud texts about Jesus' connection to us beyond death from John's accounts of the Last Supper: John 14:1-3 (I go prepare a place for you) or John 14:18-20 and 27-31 (I will come back, I will not leave you alone).
- Read sections of creeds that are important in your congregation.

Discuss how these passages and creeds interpret Mary's experience and the resurrected Jesus' presence with her.

Together, imagine what Mary would say to explain what happened on Easter and what it means for her. It may help to imagine that she is writing "The Gospel According to Mary" or that she is speaking to a group of Christians some years later.

Divide into small groups. Each group will plan a way to tell Mary's Easter story for one age: older preschoolers, younger elementary children, and older elementary students. Challenge each group to decide where to start and end and what events and ideas to include in the story. Have groups report in age sequence starting with the youngest so that everyone can trace how the themes can be developed as children grow.

In reflecting on these activities, pose the following questions for discussion:

- What was Mary's Easter surprise?
- How did that surprise affect her life?
- What does Mary's story tell our children and us about our lives and deaths?

Closing: Read aloud one of the following children's books, pondering what happens after death. Then gather up concerns of the session in prayer.
- *The Next Place* by Warren Hanson (Minneapolis: Waldman House Press, 1997)
- *The Goodbye Boat* by Mary Joslin, illustrated by Claire St. Louis Little (Grand Rapids: Eerdmans Books for Young Readers, 1999)
- *Waterbugs and Dragonflies: Explaining Death to Young Children* by Doris Stickney, illustrated by Gloria Ortiz Hernandez (Cleveland: The Pilgrim Press, 1997)

Note: This session can lead people to raise a variety of questions: "What do we tell our children about death?" "What happens when we die?" Answers to these questions fall into two categories: how we help children grieve and what we tell them about death. There are many excellent books on the former. You may want to make some of these available for interested parents. Conversations during this session may lead you to invite community experts to further explore the topic with the group. But the focus of this session needs to be on clarifying what we believe about death and resurrection and how we communicate to this to the children. Clarity on these issues helps parents respond faithfully to grieving children.

Session E: God Forgives Us

Display a cross in front of the class for this session. To open the class, point it out and note that people have been trying to explain its significance for centuries. Read the excerpt from the Confession of 1967 (The Presbyterian Church U. S. A.) from page 14. As a class, list on a board the possible interpretations of the cross that are listed in the excerpt. Challenge students to put each one into their own words. Work with this just long enough to establish that these are difficult theories and doctrines for most adults. Then note that what connects all of these explanations of the significance of the cross is forgiveness. Following the text on pages 14–15, suggest that though these theories are beyond the understanding of children, the stories from which they grew are not.

Divide the class into groups to read the biblical forgiveness texts related to the crucifixion and resurrection, and the commentaries on each from chapter 1. Ask each group to summarize its story. Use the questions for discussion below to clarify and explore the stories.

> Mark 14:27-31 and 66-72 (Peter's denial)
> John 21:1-19 (Jesus eats with Peter on the beach)
> Luke 23:39-43 (Jesus forgives a thief killed with him)
> Luke 23:32-38 (Jesus forgives those who are killing him)

Questions for discussion:
- The commentary says that the resurrection happened for Peter when Jesus dealt with his three denials by asking, "Do you love me?" three times. According to this, what is the Easter good news for Peter?
- Who does Jesus forgive in Luke 23:34? What does that tell us about God's forgiveness?
- The four texts tell of three cases of forgiveness. Which of the three speak most strongly to you? Why? Which would you expect to speak most strongly to your children? Why?
- Returning to the excerpt from the Confession of 1967 ask, "Do you agree that the stories communicate God's forgiveness on their own as well as or better than the salvation theories spun out by the church over the years? Why or why not?"

Present and discuss the information about the importance of modeling forgiveness with young preschoolers (see pages 24–25) and older children too (see pages 29–30).

Closing: Read chapters nine and ten from *Peter's First Easter*, by Walter Wangerin Jr., aloud. Close with prayer of thanksgiving for Easter forgiveness.

Session F: How We Keep Lent as a Family

Open the session by inviting students to share memories of Lent and Easter from their childhood at both home and church. Welcome all memories, the good, the bad, and the just plain odd.

Present the family disciplines in chapter 3 and others with which you are familiar. As you work through ideas, keep a running list of them on a chalkboard or newsprint. Invite students to add to the list. When the list is complete, do one of the following:

- Go through the list asking students to identify what their family would need from the congregation to try that discipline.
- Challenge each household to identify the four disciplines that look most promising for their family this year. Tally the results. Once again discuss what support families would need from the church to be successful.
- Give students a copy of the congregation's Lenten calendar. Discuss which events families are likely to participate in and why. Talk about ways the events could be made more family friendly.

Offer students a collection of family Lenten resources including devotional guides, activity books, and calendars. As the resources are passed around, hear individual comments about the strengths and weaknesses of the resources. (A list of such resources is included in part 4)

Closing: Try one of the suggested prayer disciplines. Pray through the Lord's Prayer with the leader praying one phrase then leaving silence for others to pray further on that subject, aloud or silently. Encourage the class to pray from "where they are" in this day, at the beginning of the Lent–Easter seasons, and in the world.

Session G: A Thinking Session for the Worship Committee

Ask committee members to read chapters 1 and 2 before the meeting. The information in those chapters is not essential to this discussion, but will greatly enrich it.

Together, make a list of Lent–Easter worship services in your congregation.

Assign one day of Lent–Easter to a small group or individual. Have each group or individual read the related material in chapters 3 through 9 and report to the group. Each report should include a summary of the ideas in the chapter and suggestions for meeting the needs of children in your congregation.

After hearing all of the presentations, evaluate the ideas in light of your current schedule of worship services. Use the following as starter questions:
- How well do we present the full Easter message to our children and their families in worship? Are there any parts of the story we do not tell them?
- Which services attract families with children? What is their attraction?
- How can events that do not draw children and their families be made more appropriate for and attractive to children?
- In which services are children involved as leaders? How can more children be included in the leadership of Lent–Easter worship?

Look at messages in Holy Week and Easter hymns in your hymnal and songbooks; pick out the two that they think would mean most to their children. Plan ways to incorporate them in worship.

Closing: Sing one of the following Easter hymns:
"Come, Christians, Join to Sing" (Note that people of all ages can be Christians)
"Let Us Talents and Tongues Employ" (Note that this is a good prayer for worship planning in any season, but especially for Easter)

PART FOUR

Lent–Easter Resources for Children and Their Adults

This is not intended to be a complete listing of available resources. The stories and ideas in the books listed here communicate Lent–Easter messages that we have explored as meaningful to children. There are no videos or DVDs on the list because I found none that met the criteria. In building a church program or stocking a resource center, you will want to pick and choose from additional resources. I hope that my annotations both help you understand why each resource was included and evaluate other available resources.

Retellings of the Biblical Stories

Arch Books, published by Concordia Publishing House
This popular series of paperback Bible storybooks combines rhymed stories with cartoon art. There are sixteen related to Easter. A literal understanding of atonement theology underlies all of them and is expressed directly in the text of many of the books and in the letter to parents at the end of all books. You will need to read each book to decide whether to use it. In general, I find that books about people and events not directly related to the crucifixion are more useful. The combination of rather hokey poetry, atonement language meant to be interpreted literally, and almost silly looking art can be jarring when the topic is crucifixion.

Easter A to Z: Every Letter Tells A Story, Lisa Flinn and Barbara Younger, illustrated by Patricia Ludlow (Nashville: Abingdon Press, 2002)
Tells the story of Maundy Thursday through Easter. On one side of the page is a series of letters and what they stand for. On the other is a related biblical text that is somewhat complicated for the stated age group. The art is strong and attractive. While the letters are not all memorable, kindergarteners and first-graders who are learning their letters will find it an interesting way to tell the story.

Hosanna! The Story of Palm Sunday; The Best Day Ever! The Story of Easter; Goodbye–for Now: The Story of Jesus' Return to Heaven, Patricia L. Nederveld, illustrated by Patrick Kelley (Grand Rapids: CRC Publications, 1998)
Three books for two- and three-year-olds with simple, age-appropriate renditions of each story and bright art. Each book includes a lesson plan for use at church and one simple suggestion for home use. This is the Easter set from *God Loves Me,* a series of fifty-two similar Bible storybooks. Order from www.crcpublications.org.

Peter's First Easter, Walter Wangerin, Jr., illustrated by Timothy Ladwig (Grand Rapids: Zondervan Publishing House, 2000)
Peter's story from the Last Supper through the fish fry on the beach, told in the first person with strength and warmth that will appeal to older elementary children, especially boys. The focus is on Jesus' forgiveness of Peter. Colorful, very human art adds even more strength to the text.

Sing Alleluia!: An Easter Story for Children, Daphna Flegal (Nashville: Abingdon Press, 1998)
The story of Jesus' life, death, and resurrection told in simple poetry with repeated chorus, "Sing alleluia, Sing, sing, sing, Sing alleluia for the..." The song stops when Jesus is killed but starts again when the women find the tomb empty. For ages 3–7.

The Children's Bible in 365 Stories, Mary Batchelor, illustrated by John Haysom (Oxford: Lion Publishing plc, 1995)
A fine Bible story book for elementary children, especially when read daily

with their families. Stories are very close to the biblical accounts and well expressed for children.

The Children's Illustrated Bible, stories retold by Selina Hastings, illustrated by Eric Thomas and Amy Burch (London: Dorling Kindersley Limited, 1994)
This Bible story book is designed for older elementary children. Stories are surrounded by sidebars explaining ancient customs and displaying articles featured in the story. It is a great study tool for older readers. The Lent–Easter stories are well told.

The Easter Story, retold & illustrated by Carol Heyer (Nashville: Ideals Publications, 2001)
A summary of the life of Jesus focused on Holy Week. The art is more suggestive than descriptive. There are no pictures of Jesus' face. This is a good book for elementary children trying to get the Holy Week events into chronological order.

The Easter Story, Lois Rock, illustrated by Diana Mayo (Oxford: Lion Publishing plc, 2002)
The size and cover of this little book suggest that it is for preschoolers. But the text is for elementary school children. The detailed story from Palm Sunday to the Ascension is told in understandable, unemotional language. It is a useful book for children who are adding details to their knowledge of the Holy Week stories and who are trying to get the whole story into chronological order. The art is simple and attractive.

The Easter Story, Brian Wildsmith (Eerdmans Books for Young Readers, 2000)
The Holy Week story is told through the eyes of the donkey Jesus rode into Jerusalem and who, in this book, observed the events of the week, finally carrying Jesus' body to the tomb. The art, like the text, is attractive but very distant. Many colorful angels observe all that happens. This book may be most useful for exploring the details of the story with young children while downplaying the horror.

The Family Story Bible, Ralph Milton (Louisville: Westminster John Knox Press, 1996)
This is another fine Bible story book for families to read together. It is especially suited to younger elementary children, but can be enjoyed by older children as well. It is illustrated with warm, human watercolors that give the stories a sense of reality.

Welcome Jesus! and *Good News for Jesus' Friends,* Carol Wehrheim and Betsy James (Cleveland: United Church Press, 1999)
Board books with one word, a simple phrase, and a picture to tell the Palm Sunday and Easter stories for 2–3 year-olds. Part of *The Word and Picture Books* series.

Related Easter Stories and Fables

Chicken Sunday, Patricia Polacco (New York: Philomel Books, 1992)
> Children accused of throwing eggs at the shop of an elderly Russian immigrant, and make pysanky, Russian Easter eggs, to convince him that they did not throw the eggs and to ask for odd jobs with which to earn money to buy a special Easter hat for their grandmother. The old man allows the children to sell eggs in his shop then gives them the hat. Beautiful story, beautifully illustrated. The only Easter connection is the Easter eggs. For elementary children.

Happy Easter, God, Elspeth Campbell Murphy, illustrated by Jim Lewis (Bloomington: Bethany House Publishers, 2001)
> A collection of poems about Easter day in the experience of very young children. Candy, eggs, clothes are included with church, Easter greetings, and the biblical story. For 2–4 year-olds.

Miss Fannie's Hat, Jan Karon (Augsburg Fortress Publishers, 2003)
> Miss Fannie is ninety-nine years old and has many hats, each one her favorite. When she is asked to donate one to an auction to raise money for her church she debates at length, then decides to donate her favorite Easter hat with pink roses on it. She goes to church on Easter Sunday, hatless for the first time, and finds the church ringed in pink roses planted to honor her contribution. More about generosity than Easter, but occurs at Easter time.

Petook: An Easter Story, Caryll Houselander, illustrated by Tomie de Paola (New York: Holiday House, 1988)
> A charming story with beautiful art about Petook, the rooster, who sees the Christ child watch a hen gather her chicks under her wings, then the crucifixion and resurrection. Use the subtle connections to Easter eggs to explore new life themes with older children.

Rechenka's Eggs, written and illustrated by Patricia Polacco (New York: Philomel Books, 1988)
> A charming story illustrated with beautiful folk art about an elderly woman, Babushka, who decorates Easter eggs. She takes in a wounded goose that turns over the table holding all her decorated eggs then lays patterned eggs to replace the broken ones before flying away. The eggs are the only Easter connection.

Sunrise Hill: An Easter Story of Faith, Inspiration, and Courage, Kathleen Long Bostrom (Grand Rapids: Zonderkidz, 2004)
> When Uncle Josh comes to an American frontier town, people band together to build a church. Two weeks before the Easter opening, the church burns down. With the help of ten-year-old Caleb the town realizes that even after the building burns, there is a church, Easter and new life. For elementary children.

The Easter Angels, Bob Hartman, illustrated by Tim Jonke (Oxford: Lion Publishing, 1999)

Two angels, a guardian angel and the angel of death, are sent to Jesus' tomb on Easter morning to make the announcement that surprises even them. The story tells what they do and how they respond. This is a thought provoking, artfully told story about new life for elementary children, youth and adults to ponder. Beautiful art adds strength to the story.

The Legend of the Donkey's Cross, Judy Buck-Glenn (Nashville: Abingdon Press, 2000)

Rachel is introduced to a donkey by Mr. Jefferson. He shows her the dark cross on the donkey's back and tells her the legend that says until Easter the crosses were not there. The biblical story is told in straight scripture interrupted by conversation between the two. Mr. Jefferson is clear that this is just an old story that helps us remember Jesus. For elementary children.

The Tale of Three Trees, retold by Angela Elwell Hunt, illustrated by Tim Jonke (Colorado Springs: Cook Communications, 2004)

Three trees dream of becoming a treasure chest, a ship, and a tree on the top of a high mountain. All get their wish, but not in the way they expect, in the life of Jesus.

The Very Hungry Caterpillar, Eric Carle (New York: Philomel Books, 1994)

A board book in which a caterpillar eats lots of vegetation on his way to becoming a butterfly. Good introduction to butterfly life cycle for preschoolers. Adults will have to make the Easter connection.

They Followed A Bright Star, Joan Alavedra, illustrated by Ulises Wensell (New York: G. P. Putnam's Sons, 1994)

As the shepherds go to the stable on Christmas, they meet others who saw angels. One is to keep a well, another to fish, another to plant grain, another to make wine that the child will need on another night of miracles. Older children recognize the Lenten events at which Jesus will use these things.

Classroom Resources and Easter Activity Books

Easter Hunt: A Hide and Seek Story, Sarah Reid Chisholm (Minneapolis: Augsburg Fortress, 1994)

A mom hides objects with which to tell the Easter story. Each page tells one Holy Week story and challenges children to find the hidden object in the picture. The story is a wonderful account for preschoolers. Finding the hidden objects will be challenging for them.

Easter Stories, Julie Elliott (Wood Lake Publishing, distributed in USA by Pilgrim Press)

A kit including a video and book of seven session plans for children ages 3–10 and/or whole congregations based on *The Family Story Bible.* The video features costumed storytellers telling the Holy Week stories in a variety of ways.

Seasons of God's Love: The Church Year, Jeanne S. Fogle, illustrated by Bea
Weidner (Philadelphia: Geneva Press, 1988)
Brief descriptions of the seasons of the church year. Lent is a time to "remember God's love." Easter celebrates the resurrection that is "God's way of
telling us that if we have faith in God, we have a new kind of life. We know
that God loves us and will be with us forever."

*Things to Make and Do for Lent and Easter: Creative Activities for Children's
Ministry,* Martha Bettis Gee (Louisvillle: Bridge Resources, 1998)
Exactly what it says, a collection of activities for children with simple direc-
tions. No suggestions about how to use them to communicate meaning.

Family Devotion and Activity Books

Before and After Easter: Activities and Ideas for Lent to Pentecost, Debbie
Trafton O'Neal, illustrated by David Larochelle (Minneapolis: Augsburg
Fortress, 2001)
Multitude of activities suggested for each day of Lent following weekly
themes: prayer, symbols, service, worship, biblical journeys, and Holy Week.
Easter to Pentecost offers only one Easter activity for each week. Families
could be overwhelmed by suggestions and would benefit from directions on
how to choose and use activities that fit them. This may be most useful as a
source of classroom activities for church school teachers.

Creative Communications for the Parish, Inc. (creativecommunications.com)
Each year this organization produces fresh children's devotional books, calendars, and family activity books for Lent, as well as resources for other age
groups. They are inexpensive and intended for mass distribution by congregations. The quality of the content varies because it is aimed for mass appeal.
But it's worth checking out each year.

Family Countdown to Easter: A Day-by-Day Celebration, Debbie Trafton
O'Neal, illustrated by Viki Woodworth (Mineapolis: Augsburg Fortress,
1998)
This book, by the author of *Before and After Easter,* includes only one activity
for each day of Lent. A sticker calendar has been added. The biblical connection has been minimized leaving a collection of activities vaguely connected to Christian faith.

EPILOGUE

Easter is indeed Good News for children. And it is our joy and also our baptismal responsibility to share it with them and to include them in the congregation's celebration of Easter. To do this we must know the stories well and know how children hear them at different ages. And we must plan ways of introducing the children to and including them in the Lenten disciplines and events with which we celebrate the season. This requires thoughtful attention on the part of parents, teachers, pastors, and congregational planners. It also requires energy. Still, it has been my experience that when the thought is taken and energy expended, the children are well served and God offers yet another Easter surprise. Our adult experience and understanding of the holy season are deeply enriched as well.